Time Capsule

by

Ideas with Ink

101 Panya Publishing
101panya@gmail.com
ISBN-10: 1-988880-01-7
ISBN-13: 978-1-988880-01-3
BISAC: POE011000

Table of Contents

Existence

He is a stranger to summer for his heart lies in
winter.

Blue

We are all blue,
But we wear glasses.
Some wear red ones,
As if we were bruised.

Some wear yellow ones,
As if we were rooted.
Some wear white ones,
As if we were winged.

Some wear blue ones,
As we are blue.

Sailing

Alone in a sea of people
I swim through the crowd,
Through the broken glass beach
Of my dreams.

The sky is naked and the rain
Embittered.
The winter stripped the trees
and put them to sleep.

The night hushed the wolf,
The mare,
The sun.
It stole the light of the moon and stars

In the darkness, I master her fire.
Her smile, her little vessel,
Guides me to the leafy isles of her soul.

Those Who Live

Those who dance on the stage of Life,
Those who sing in alabaster coats,

Those who paint the Creator and His Creations,
Those who write about first loves and of eternal
longing,

Those who live in God's reflections, on sun kissed
soil,
Those who sleep in His ocean beds.

Eyes that open,
Eyes that close.

Mourning

Child warmed by love
Never shivers in my heart's obscurity.
Covered in ash
The blood trickles from my heart
Into yours.

Dearest Boy,
Climb from the waters
Where death left you.
Look for our home,
Draped in the blue of my tears,
Which will whiten in your presence.

The trees asleep in winter's magic
Will bring forth apples
As golden as your smiles.
Hummingbirds will flutter to your voice
As if the voice of spring.

Do not look for algae that
Blooms on the brinks of seas,
Or the bright long strays of the sun,
But for golden hair in the wind.

Do not search for
Fires that breathe in the dry winter air,
Or for crosses in the skies,
But for my warmth.

My arms will embrace you,
My lips will kiss you on your soft cheeks.
Place your heart on mine

I am an old fruitless tree,
Or a flowerless field.

You are to me
Like a star to the sky.

Feel

Earth of heart,
Water of soul,
Fire of eyes,
Air of Freedom.

Earth's Sky

The sun paints its golden radiance in the sky.
An obscure moon gives birth to a thousand stars.
Earth, sickly, sleeps like a child in the midst of
winter.

Winter in my Heart

It was winter in my heart, in my life.
I was on the boat, a party on board,
But friends turn foes.

I wait here on an island,
Blue trees, snow pattering.
I look onto the sea:
The ice lowly retreats,
But my binoculars are foggy
My compass not to tell North from South
Not to say, whether the saviors were
From the East,
From hope or West foes.

I lie hidden until the man in a white suit departs.
A maiden wearing a green dress is left.
She wipes the fog off and leads me uphill.
I look from the top,
A small skiff comes towards me.

I get dressed as a sign for the lady to leave,
White flocks to come down again.
She rushes to the shore with them.
The boat vanishes.

I do not

I do not see the mountains that glow of iron,
Iron that my soul hungers for,
Or the moon that burns like a candle
Above rows and rows of stars.

I do not hear the trees whisper of you and me.
The fire burns the sonnet,
The night roars like a panther,
Hunting for the gazelle of my dream.

I do not feel your breast in my hands,
Your peachy lips on my lips,
Or even your fire in my soul.
Like the wind that follows the butterfly,
Like the child trails a mother,
You guide me from the intoxicating pines,
From the sea of glass,
From the dark cedar groves of my childhood
To the zenith where I grow faster than before,
Where earth and sky coalesce,
Where love brings us garlands of kisses and
marigolds.

In You the Change

Underneath your feet -
The road's dynamo
Of white butterflies
Electrocutes bleak isles
Where women of the sea
Trod on velvet, machetes.

Here, my people
Emerged from a poppy,
Wingless, yet in flight
There, a shadowy mountain,
As if the star's saddle
Beneath the winepress night
Grind their moon into quartz.

Here, my eyes' net
Of maritime days,
A dove asleep
As if the earth at twilight
That adores
Our little bees:
Seeps, seizes, sieges.
From the honeyed pubis
Beyond, nights
Go on to drown each other.

The sky is
Overburdened with dreams.
On your lips, a crane dies.
The paper crane is born in my palm.
Here, winter climaxes on spring.
Stars chase
One another for crystal-laughter.

Shipwrecked Shadow

We are all made of rain.
Shadows under the guise
Of humans.
Sell voices
In destiny's marketplace,
Buy ourselves from
Ourselves.
Dream
About shipwrecks.

Rotation, Revelation

Earth spins
The tin moon
Between:
Phony
Stargazers,
Nocturnal
Suns,
Sleeping
Dreams.

Earth's Cape

The earth is a cape of lamps
Of the mountain bride.
Everything mounts
On shadowy vessels
Of smiles,
But my voice:
Diggs graves in
Life's depths,
Drowns
In twilight's
Bed sheets.

Goodbye

He said goodbye to day and night,
Darkness and Light,
Freedom and Fight.

Searching

In the simple night
My soul searches for your fire.
Your song, as if the wind,
Travels through my ailing body.

From my quay your
Majestic galleon departed
Until death, as if the wind,
Drove you to the drunken coasts of life.

I circle the unyielding winds,
The never-ending horizon.
I hold the mother-like hand of the air,
The smoke covers my shameful face.

I walk on destiny's path
Without the impalpable star of love
Until the destitute leaves of autumn
Cover the ashes of my faithful heart.

Freedom

Under fallen stars, she slumbers,
Under the hushed rustle of autumn.

Empty as the skies of winter,
Full as the day where love met her.

Simple in possession as spring,
Rich in valour and spirit as a hymn.

Neither asleep, nor awake.
One hand full of golden chaff,
Another reaches for the splendours of the sky.

She listens to the church rhythm
And nature's pulse,
Gently succumbs to the woes of life.

Half-Bloodied Moon

I.

We hung tinsel stars
Upon the gallows of our mouths
In their thistle fedoras,
And my phosphoric lighters
Infiltrated your ashtray womb
Among the phantoms of cocottes,
Who plotted to become nuns,
Heaving as if unleavened insomnia
Trickling into cots of POWs (Prisoners' of War).

II.

Infinitesimal night emancipates
Our silhouettes atop the chalky path
Belfries penetrating virgin skies
Droplets of a wine thrice drank
Once by a rosy infant of the bordello,
Once by a vain king of rooks, pawns,
Once by a lamplighter,
Who draped the world in blood
And smeared acid across
Dew-smattered secrets.

III.

Diadem of windowpanes,
Bruise maiden vending pleated sofas
Barefoot in cherry-cola's ridges
With a dozen planetary eyes
And a torn heart
Undulating as a carillon;
On her bracing hips
Clusters of servile ravens
Marooned within centipede bowties.

IV.
Shipwrecks of hearts,
MDNA (Madonna) walleyes, gills of euphoria
Capsize into my bitter Americano
Encircled by a quartered earthenware seawall.
The key of B reeks of brine.
Your net of kisses cannot
Encapsulate my soul's shadowy train.
We are, but Davids, inky blood.
Our arms: foamy anvils.
A hymn of wells
Submerges the vagrant stars
Without doors or windows,

With an eternity of padlocks
Drawn from firebirds, parasols, consciences.

Sell the World

The night bleeds stars,
Earth is a hospital.

There is a sale on sails
To reach the profit-prophet.

Some days I want to jump
Out of my eyes

And spend my life
In an atlas.

Falling

Rainfall,
Nightfall,
Snowfall,
Dewfall,
Rainfall.

Stroke

You paint my heart blue -
I drown.

You paint it orange -
And I burn.

You paint it white -
And I freeze.

You draw in my mind -
I erase.

Shadows and Reflections

His body lies in the black crepe of night,
In a bed of rocks in river of tears.

His mind is drunk with fame's wine,
Tainted with your love,
Shivered like the trees in winter
In a hideaway, in the nation's soul.

His soul, tinged with night,
Flutters as a little butterfly
In the endless sands of sin.

He danced to the sunrise,
Sung with the sparrows,
Listened with passion to the sunset's ode.

It was once figments,
But he made it a reality.
The children of life
Showed him that Earth
Dreamt of sparrows.

The young maiden of the morning
Fantasizes of sunrises.
The little stars that shimmer at twilight
Dream of sunsets.

But God dreams of all and created all:
The sparrows, the sunrises, and sunsets
He gave life to Mother Nature,
The Morning Maiden,
The Dancing Stars,
Invented Love, Beauty, Nature -

All God's reflections,
Where He looks to Himself.

But under each reflection
Lies a shadow of
Vanity, Ugliness,
A place that God neglects.

For every flicker of beauty
Lies a candle of vices.
For every dream of His -
A nightmare shudders His mind.
For every picture shot -
One vanishes.
For every life given -
One disappears.

The night erases all the remnants
Of the hopeless man,
Of the dreamless man.

All That Remains is a Voice

All that remains is a voice,
That crumbles into thousands of dreams
Atop sea of tears.

Two white eyes seek refuge,
Fly as larks to rest
On the moon's shadowy, silvery breast.

An Island in a Sea of People

Through orange orchards they trotted,
Through clear streams we waded.
It was the summer of our life,
Even in the winter storm,
The summer of allure, of camaraderie,

But it lacked something,
It provided our basic needs, food and water.
With Serenity and Friendship
It gave us breath and a heart beat,
But the soul shivered.

Up on a plateau,
One hundred steps
Lays a stream.
He ran to quench the thirst of his soul,
Drunk from it.
The water gave life,
Bold shadows and vivid reflections.
Without it our eyes would not wet,
Our body would not shake.

Are we not human?
Can we not bleed like Jesus?
We still love as we did.
We still hate.
The body hasn't changed,
But only the mind
We feel fear and sadness differently.
Our sweat, blood and tears - the same.
It fuelled not only the bulbs, but the roots.
The eyes saw the water entered the lips.
The heart - into the soul.

A vast sea of tears and a drop of blood
Poses guilt on the seas,
Or when in the heart of the night
A little light brings back day.

The water reminded him of his youth,
But age takes all.
His body began to lack splendour and strength.
Looks, Wealth are horses, but Integrity,
Grit, a dog rubbing your legs.
Then came a deluge,
Vast floods.
On the island with the man, his dog and horses
Came a pack of wolves and a clan of serpents.

The beauty left with the horses in the deep of the
night,
But the dog stood beside him, a warrior,
Attacked the wolves, but he fell at their mercy.
His carcass dropped into a pool of blood.
He became one with his master.

His master gained his inner flame.
The wolves surrounded him.
Moved ever so close, waited to pounce.
The end in the skies.
He defended himself.
Set death upon the pack.
He reached the serpent's lair
One by one death became them,
But alas one serpent hidden upon rocks,
Stroked from behind with a mortal blow.
The man turned,

Clutched the serpent's neck,
Knew the path is at its end.
Compassion overtook him,
He set him free.

The serpent walked into the water,
Disappeared under the waves.
The soul in his body has awoken.
He remembered the master, his dog,
How even in a sea of people
One can shudder alone on an island.
He bade farewell,
Began the journey home.

Union (I)

Earth serves us
Divorce papers.

Then, Saturn
Is the ring bearer.

We are islands,
Boats fissured with longing.

We are countries
Bordered with destiny.

Tie your future to mine,
We will weave banners of life.

Everyone is caught
In the dream catcher
Of themselves.

Death Came Out of Autumn's Closet

We are murderers
Since we kill time.

Clocks wear our hands,
Rivers sing with your mouth.

The stars
Are
Dream
Catchers.

I have never ventured within
An airport, but for your eyes.
I lived in myself till
I found myself.

Dead City

We are waterproof
To happiness.

Your eyes are lonely mills
That churn tears.

A city sprouts from your chest,
Nobody lives there.

We are all named Nobody.
You came from the nothingness
Since you made everything

Spring swallowed the moon
Before dreaming.

River Besieging Nazareth

I.
My soul is an inkwell
Among shadowy proxies.
Eternities of Skype calls
Coagulate on the unfurling
Book of brine with understudies
Of suicidal waves.
A dove for each page-break,
A bloodstain for each inquiry
Shivers in sandy bosoms

II.
Your name in smoky syllables
The drunkard consumed for Passover.
Atop the thorny Via Dolorosa
Jesters with the muddled laughter
Of a tree whose trunk encapsulated
An obituary of our love (and my crystal timepiece)
Within the golden chapel, Peddlers
Gorged on starry cornbread, crusty horizons.

III.
Our roots entwined the pew.
Great anthems of light rising
From shady hymnals, which my sister ignited
Last Wednesday allied with Goring's phantom.

IV.
We stole matches,
Ate poppies from the row of crosses.
Our arms coalesced into them after.
Crows gagged the scarecrow-
A ligature of ant queens

Nuptial wombs of hushed foragers
Fled Rasputin's honeyed globe,
A lone weaver on the looms of dawn,
An undone love in a zipper of husks.

V.
Oblivion dressed like a seamstress
Impregnated with misery.
Death - that humiliated supervisor
When the weaver only jarred
Tulips with bruised panniers,
Oily kisses; She was rootless.
We existed in tubers of laughs
In each others' hearts of cards.
Vermillion king on snowy deathbed
Our love performed euthanasia
To become despair.

VI.
Toasts become dreamy butterflies.
The world is a carousel
And stars - those dingy mares
Wafting tune: spring's wakeup call
To chisel marble effigies of clouds
And dissolve her green eyes
Into rivers of sprigs
With an isle of an admiral and a debutante
Infatuated beneath inky skies the comet-poet
Pondered about while in slumber
Juxtapositions of Abstractions.

Wind that pimps a butterfly
Toward abstinent windows
Taciturn bridges moored onto sunned skies.
Here, Death loved you.

Mother-of-pearl street-lamps
Among twilight's transient foam-veins
Blue-eyed river of semen, mirrors.
My brother enthralled with himself.

Poppies reunited within syringes.
Wombs of ashtrays, hearts of tiny cowbells,
Emporiums vending syllables, prosthetics, breath.
My daughter seduced by a mannequin.
Train-wrecked heart
In a cool underpass of penuries.
Souls dissolve into silhouettes atop sundials.
My mother courts a phantom.

Vivacious flower
Asleep in oblivion's jar
Resurrected into shadowy honey.
I loved an effigy.
I smelled of jasmine,
brine,
you.

The Earth/La Tierra

I do not look for heavenly constellations,
Like you, my Lady
But on earth, my earth
The smooth skin of
bread
The eyes of the fountain,
shiny coins
Trees with crowns of
Leaves and forbidden fruit
The sea with hair
Twisted like a princess
But you are mine
Some shine more,
Some have a longer stride
But you are mine
In your heart there is a country
Where there are no tears
And loneliness
Drunken by spruces
Saddened by the infinity of galaxies
The departure of me,
In my beach
Of remorse
On a boat of Basalt
Laden with kisses and flowers
Sailing over lakes of your tears
For your island, your soul
Where I am like a tree
I grow my roots in your soul
Bring me your water, your thoughts, your words
And I protect you with my shadow
Of those who blacken you
And paint you, violet

The Earth/La Tierra (Spanish)

Yo no miro por constelaciones divinos,
Como tú, mi Señora
Pero, sobre la tierra, mi tierra
La piel lisa del pan
Los ojos de la fuente,
Monedas relucientes
Por ti, no por usted
Los árboles con las coronas
De Hojas y la Fruta prohibido
El mar con el pelo
Trenzado como una princesa
Pero tú eres mío
Algunos brillan más,
Algunos tienen una zancada más larga
Pero tú eres mío
En tu corazón hay un país
Donde, no hay lágrimas
Y soledad
Borracho, por las piceas
Entristecen, por el infinito de las galaxias
La partida de mí,
En mi playa
Del remordimiento
En un barco del basalto
Agobiado con los besos y flores
Navegaba encima de lagos del lágrimas
Para tu isla, tu alma
Donde yo soy como un árbol
Crezco mis raíces en tu alma
Trae a mí, tu agua, tus ideas, tus palabras
Y protejo tú, con mi sombra
De los que ennegrecen tú
Y pintan tú, violeta

Chaff

The stars tinge the never-ending sky
The moon wakes and enables her waves
And you rest on a foam-laden cliff
In a diadem of inebriated stars.

O, lonely rose enacting tears,
Dreams draped in sad suits of light.

The butterfly unstoppable by freedom
Perches on the naked trees of winter.

Abyss filled with life,
Silence with sound.

The nameless wind razes lighthouses
The incessant sea paves forests of flowers with
sand.

Here, you bring forth the only infinite love
In the form of blue crystals and thistles,
Flowerless, flightless, full of life.

Creed

We are a clan of stoic beings,
Even our tears glow of mercury.
A wolf runs in our screams,
Stone lips and hearts.

Only she truly feels
She is the tree,
Rustles like the rain.
The river alone as an orphan.

Cut with our machetes,
Bruised with our footsteps
She falls into a coma,
White, bitter, deathlike.

We resurrect her as if our saviour
With slaughtering hands,
Hands that end in the wrong places:
In her violet lips, mountain breasts.

She walks toward death,
With narcotics
Of sodium and sulphur.
Only her soul the sun,
Our hands will never feel.

Observations of the Night

The silver river sings her children verses,
The savage wind drives her to the sea,
Leaves her drunken with brine,
Cut by basalt.

The train gains her freedom,
Death drives her into the embittered pine forest.

The moon undresses herself.
The night steals her whites.

Low Spirits

My dream is a vagrant wind,
That rustles the autumn leaves like a train.

The long industrious night tinges the sufferer of my
soul.
Desert sand fills my oblivious mind.

Fires no longer warm me.
Water only thirsts me.

I shall see my father lying in the river.
My mother shall sing to me in the skies.

My soul is a silver church
Without the cross of your resonant star.

My suffering seeps into the soil.
My longing sails into the skies.

I shall humbly rest under the earth's golden glow
Like an ocean waiting for your serenade of stars.

Separation

The forlorn trees dance in the wind's song.
I will dream of spring on the autumn leaves.

You will thread them, brumal rose, warm home,
The decaying hand of life will guide me to your fire.

You are the word *morose*.
A naked tree.

I will wade in the waters of death in search for your.
Eyes as if sunken diamonds, forgotten dreams

I create a vessel of flotsam and flowers.
We will glide faster than day.

But Death will edge closer
Like a teary-eyed river.

It separates your sinking heart
From my sleeping body.

Flowers

Your lips open; a dew crowned rose,
Laced with dream, nude.
Sweet words rain on my bare chest
In the form of light hidden in wild violets.

Queen of the forgotten dawn,
Blue, twisted slave of the shattered night
Dancing like wheat with stars!

The earth throbs in bird-filled reveries.
Waves sleep on foam beds.
Beneath the lighthouse-like cliff
Stars disentangle from their light-hued garb.

The moon bleeds streams of silver, finite dreams.
My heart closes in streaks of ice.
A river that never reaches the sea,
Sleeps on a pillow, a moonlike slab of basalt,
Drunken on loneliness.

Only Mountains Live Forever

The song: the wind cooing the sun
Amid the green avenues of pine
And of waves crashing against the isles of
melancholy.
The sight of your brows intoxicated on freedom and
brine
Flying as dreams atop the teary-eyed sea
And your ever changing white eyes,
As if larks leaving the green and blue
For the moon's silvery shadowy cliff.

In the night void of life from mountain to sea,
I knit the words among your stars of hope
On the dew of the newfound spring.
I walk rootless around the earth
For another peek of my childhood land
Peopled with the echo of laughter
And the sea of bleeding poppies.

The song lives and dies with the birth
And demise of my memories,
So I bequeath to you dark, sonorous lover, my dreams,
Which live in your hazel tree-eyes.
What a dream, what a land!
Hidden grove of love, deep green stream of secrets.

You with your little blue eyes lived on the moon
The crazy-eyed men were wading in the livid river of
death! They had come with snared lips and dark
hearts.
They took our land and when I said no
They pushed harder, mutilating every little flower
Including the thorny roses.

They walked away with their sad perverted minds
Toward life, death, twisted happiness, hidden
melancholiness.
They didn't find love in a field of flowers
But in the metallic city of men.
I discovered a white pure snow in you for my void.

Where were you, Ariane, on which planet,
On which mountain?
Were you a figment of my gray mind?
No, no you were the little blue bell,
That rung the solace in the appearing mirage.

In that instant, that little moment
You became the fire that lit my life.
You brought earth, air and water.
I dug through the layers of dirt, of hellos and
goodbyes
To find your desolate amethyst cove.

Your sweet songbird voice filled the air with lullabies.
Your little dreamy mind lives among sweet clouds.
Your winged soul flew through the sealed skies
With its infinite love to exist among golden-eyed stars
And an omniscient moon.

My world is empty for all I attained, felt, lived and
died, in you. My dreams as birds perched on the cleft
of your soul.
My words crashed into your heart as derailed trains
Laden with broken hopes.
The flowers of love grew in the water of your song;
The salt of my tears coalesced into little crystals
Nestled on your oceanic lap.

My girl painted of pen and born of paper,

With your deep pallor and padlock of solitude,
Left so seamlessly from our bed of love
Into the garden of glass beneath.
You took, Ariane, the hidden light
As candid as the lighthouse's dream
That lived in the gentle rose, which sealed your lips.

Cemetery of solitude, words still fly onto heaven's
gate
And write themselves on the northern sky.
Your whisper snows onto my sad smile,
Weighs it down into a frown.
Perhaps only the butterfly leaves with her dreams
intact,
That the caterpillar-train of anguish becomes a kite of
bliss.

Hungry ravenous lovers embrace each other by the
pines.
His bliss tastes the honey of her lips
And her fantasy – the warm bread of his mouth.

My sorrow as a great sea drowns the vessel of kisses.
You are far, tremble among sad stars.
Your green eyes above illuminate my forest of solace.
You undermine spring, little carillon of a bluebell
That penetrates the snow of oblivion
And whose ringing brings ice-cast statues to life,
When you live among nuptial dreams and forgotten
souls.
You, Ariane, are not forgotten,
But live in the flowerbeds of my thoughts,
A little butterfly on the tip of my tongue!

Everything that grew in your soul died in my heart,
The intoxicated marigolds, the lap of fading topaz.

Except, the trembling shadows that draw in letters of
chalk, Dark phrases, cool soul guides my warm hand,
my silent voice.
It has no leaps and bounds, travels through the cave of
echoes,
On the Via Dolorosa and the labyrinth of deep
restlessness!
The song that rises from my mouth into your large
blue eyes
As if fish into a deep ocean.
I live in the cage of darkness.
Only music can pierce your soul, your wildflower
filled isle.

In the night void of life spreads from mountain to sea.
I knit the words from your stars of hope
And the dew of the newfound spring.
I walk rootless around the earth for another peek
Of my childhood land peopled with the echo of
laughter
And the sea of withered poppies.

The song lives and dies with the birth
And demise of my memories.
I bequeath, to you dark, sonorous lover, my dreams,
Which exist in your hazel tree-eyes.

My dream is a butterfly in its coat of rain
On the last night of autumn.
My love is a caterpillar in its jacket of dew
On the first spring morning.

An Ode to Ariane

Ariane: A dream, a fire, a butterfly.
Your lips were boats of roses.
Hair - the fire of life.

The voice of spring, of freedom
Laden with the aromas of pines,
Sounded like one dove cooing another.

I fell into your soul,
Into the chasm of a dream.

Your blood
As if an endless army brought happiness
To the stronghold of oblivion
In the depths of my heart.

My blue, tearful world faded into
Bright shades of scarlet skies,
Emerald forests.

Sunlight entered the gate
Of your amber necklace.
Your rose fell into
My soul's garden.

But your eyes didn't gaze on my isle,
My ocean.
They longed for him

Your thoughts, paper airplanes,
Found refuge

In the green ink letters
Of his notes.

Two blue flowers of those eyes
Slept on the plain of his chest.
Your heart's star electrified his soul,
Left in me the violet darkness.

Sorrow drowns my vessel of kisses.
My butterfly doesn't
Perch next to yours
On the cherry tree of love.

The painted moon
Sleeps in the silver,
Dreamy cedar.

To a Tree

I could love a tree:
They are rooted like me,
Entwined with aloof rings
With morphine butterflies.

We could never ensconce the earth
Not through running, dying or dreaming.

If the world was an atlas
I would have abandoned it, grimy
Atop the sky's inky armoire.

I, encapsulated in her trunk,
As if an echo in a domineering cavern
With all my vinyls, geodes, tubers.
She: an overpass over my heart's
Poppy-ravaged gorge.

To a Spring

Little tassels of sprigs
With a thousand moist eyes.

Hips of my echoing homeland,
Heaving padlocks to vulnerable stars.

Closed like a flower
Amidst mercenaries of snow.
Impounded petals.
Thieving stamens.

You are the Libra,
Bosom of discarded eviction-notices,
In the opaque chaos of shadows,
In icicles sedating rivers.

To Blood

A blood-clod
Within the Red Sea,
Where the vermillion ruler
Dealt Russian roulette to jets
Of rusted mouths.

Agape mines wore
The green-lurching tremors
Amidst devilish axes
That betrayed their
Pine-mothers with whiskers.

Resin coagulated
Into shadowy honey,
Amber diadem
For the nuptial ant-queen.

The Birch Tree

The light dances on your leaves,
In your timid shadow it sleeps

Your leaves are drunk with sunshine,
With the scent of spring

O, birch tree, birch tree!
It is through your eyes I see the world.
It is your trunk that I caress.
It is, as if your roots keep me here.

Your bark is like the city gates,
The key to your soul,
To your leaves,
To your little eyes
Imprinted on your skin.

One day I saw a spectacle,
As you permeated the sky.
The sea embraced you,
Birch Tree

Every day our eyes met,
Maiden in a rose coat,
In a beret of butterflies.
We waltzed around
As you danced with the wind.

She vanished and left her child
As we flew with the sparrows
Basked in the sun's glow,
But the summer child left me too

We meet again.

But now you are faded,
Wrapped a coat of oblivion.
Your soul has become impalpable,
Your body vagrant

The trees despise you:
You separated them
From their possessions,
Lady Autumn.

But you spare those leaves,
Dancing Leaves,
As the trees lose
What they value most,
You are separated
From the forum
Of life and love.

For the ogre of winter
Banishes all in her trunk
In winter the leaves
Still linger on you.

From the woodpecker opening
We see her comrades part
For the men murder them.

Through the panes
We see them stand for another night
With seemingly more life
Than in you, birch tree.

When dusk brings day
They are only corpses
But from the corpses sprout their children.

As the ice retreats
We parade through the trees,
The birch fosters the young,
Born in winter.

Dreams Soaked in Purple Rain

The day bestowed me the right to live,
The sun to love,
The sky to dream,
The moon to feel,
The stars to remember.

Silence is murdered by a chorus.
Darkness - by rows of lights.
Emptiness - with a kiss
From the girl under the snow.
Soberness - with the scent of an evergreen.

Lonely paths
Covered footsteps
Shivering dreams,
Frozen souls.

In the empty sky a star shines.
On the tree one leaf stands.
In the child's chorus an angel sings among.

Your heavenly voice
Guides me past temptresses,
Gold coins,
Past paradise
Warm bright city lights
Into a shadow where a rose weeps,
As we fall from it into the night sky,
Collect stars,
Sleep, weep on moon rock,
Encircle the sun.

The sunrise comes -
I sent you on the last comet
To a distant planet,
To sleep in violets,
To be dressed in violet.

Purple rain, shade of sad beauty,
Washes your soul
With anguish and tenderness.

The Stars

The Stars are

Measuring spoons
For infinity,

Stopwatches
To eternity,

Highways
To voices,

Tolls
For silence,

Prisons
For dreams,

Halfway-houses
To souls.

Starfish

Stars burned.
Oceans drowned.

The moon discarded
Her jar of despair
Onto the bird keeper
To Miracles.

Stars drowned.
Oceans burned.

Earth's Guitar is out of Tune

Night is a vending machine
Of stars.
Infinity caged you.
You encaged infinity.

Endless sidewalks lead to a kiss.
Only the highway snakes to solitude.
Two dreamers dream one dream.
One dreamer dreams two dreams.

You plant glass flowers.
In the moon's jar.
I refund my happiness
For an unused heart.

Riverbed

Beds sail
From the sea of people
Into the ocean of tears;
We drown in the bed sheets.

The world is a dead fish
Full of tear-salt
In the star-net
Of the fisherman
Casting dreams
To dreamers.

Flowering Hour

Neither the crystal tides,
Nor the quartz moon could submerge
The night's most luminous souls
Or the sunrise line of your brows
In hours unfastened like roses,
Spaciously divided into seagulls.

My life grows thirsty
Without your laughter.
Your feet run through the
Gates of my oceanic eyes
Into the shadowy mouth
Of my dream
As if dew.

I undress your words for
The world to revive.
I plant five flowers
On my chest, on my glass chest
To kiss the earth and sprout
Through your eyes,
To mill honey into
Kisses.

Trains Running in My Dream

The trains are all asleep
In the embittered pine forest.
Windows disentangle themselves
From their ashen coats
Boreas assailed in twilight's grate.

The moon extinguishes her cigarette of a still comet.
A star descends into the cesspool of anguish, pinot.
The night weaves garlands of clouds,
Crowns the snowy, implacable hills.

All flesh, life is in deep slumber
From the mountain to the lake,
All but you, me, us on the vagrant rails

Axles inscrutably spin the sky into a coat of solitude
Gears morph clouds into air-flowers.
Are we but butterflies flitting,
In the spring-like smog,
Past the amber-paned sky,
And the tinsel sun?

The train of dreams departs the station of my eyes
And enters your soul.
Here melancholy coagulates
In lost keys to April's coveted light,
Lapses coins to night's vending machine of dreams:
Water's smile
The pendant of a bluebell
Autumnal roots.

The switchman is a tea-brewer of
Verdant dreams.

The absurd world is but a pre-loved kettle.
The womb's water - kerosene of childhood days.
Spray of the tulip-barge approaches the
Peachy horizon.
Throbbing sparks as
Rootless,
Flower-intoxicated
Star-burgeoning
Trains
Rain into your
Gaping mouth.

Our lips coalesce
Into the sole mass of an
Unopened,
Bullet-riddled
Kiss
And an infinite
Track of laughter.

The Crazy Night Drowns in Your Tears

Running into everyone
I fall into you.

The moon discards her
Jar of miracles in the despair.

Night is a saddle
For our abandoned dreams.

Here, there:
Cemeteries of silenced objects
Gallop on the coast of your lips.

You mine my life's depths with
An extinguished star.

Because Night Collapses On Our Dreams

Because night collapses
On our dreams
You make the struggle
From mountains.

The moon mills voices
Mines eyes.
It dances in stillness.
We sing in silence.

You make my life
With earth,
From a birdcage
Without any birds.

There are no Dreams

There are no dreams
Or dreamers,
Nothing,
Nobody,
Nothing.

The moon is a carillon
Of my voice which is
Made of every voice.
Earth is a chipped glass
In rain's dishwasher

Since you are everything
I am nothing.
I am forged from you.
You arrived from nobody
And lived in everybody.

Nothing,
Nobody,
Nothing.
In the depths of your life
Everybody knocked.

Comber

Every spring
Of each hour
Of diurnal dreams
Dissever into
The stars' clods of blood
Coalesce as azure crystals
Into sullen bluebells, wicks;
Throughout the tallowed sky
Slaughterers in coronets of bones.

I paced through
Voice and silence,
Dream and haze,
Initiations and divergences,
Past manors who heaped
Cigarette-ash
Of taciturn comets,
Winey embraces of
Inebriated inkwells.

From the sea of weeping
Tides of anguish engulf
The silver penitentiary of my heart,
Encase twilight's butterflies.

Blue, macabre glints
Of rigidity's iron
Rift from lightning's
Lie-cleaved board
Into multitudes
Of uncertainties

You were a firebird
Of autumn's fronds
In my verdant soul
A dove in a mercenary's
Viridescent eyes.
The word: forsaken,
In garlands of caresses.

A glass panther traverse infernos
Of groins, heated hearts, autumnal hearths
Assail the train of shadows
That billows as a morphine syringe
In the soporific chapel of euphoria
Honed on hallucinations, poppy-hewn lips.

Comatose veins of phosphorus,
Bleeding moons,
Erect courgettes
Are, but the spume
Of a kaleidoscopic dream.

Love's form in the flute,
Of risen baguettes vended
To arrogant duchesses of tulle
In spines of voyageurs
On the archipelago of Serendipity,
Chrysalis of Pomona's oak crucifix
Of an unabridged lap
Errant pupae of oblivion.

Each lover with
Eyes of mourning
And a cot of scalded tongues
Curbed slurs,
Montages of roses

And their clockwork lurch,
Chèvre of
The sleet-clad mountain.

A nectarine of the sky
With its earthy pit of solitude,
The alley's bosom of rolls
Unleavened with insomnia,
Transcendences of
Despondent kilns
Diadems of ash.

Heart of thorny goblets
Singes the mouth's
Underpass of cold leaves
Thickets unify within
Orations of dew, bitterness
Divulged by the vagrant fuse
That muzzles vacant souls,
Amidst a scuffling of spiders
And their silk-works.

They pitied love with bruises
White, solemn tributary
With bedrock of rosy infants.

Mourning Lighthouses

Dream as if a lost child.
By the fermented seaside
Encase memories as if shells.

Hands run into rivers
Of vertical salt amongst geysers.
Great watery laughter twisted
To the eyes' starry void.

Shadows beckon the horizon
Within grilles of clouds.
Mourners of the caravan and autumn
Hiss, froth, deliberate.

I am the lighthouse of darkness.

Between Silhouettes

I.
Amidst echoing, graphitized pines
Fire ants gag oblivion's jar,
Gift their Queen
Granulated, bruised diadems.

II.
Foamy wombs where the sea
Still throbs, black and white
A lighthouse brings forth
Daughter of hope, thistle beret.

III.
My heart is a river of song
Within your atlas of miracles,
In the rafters of despairs,
Beneath the gutters
Of high stars,
The padlocks of our mouth.

IV.
The trains of rhythm ensconce
Fervent springs,
Undress to tunnels
Of nude fortepianos,
In brisk symphonies of flour,
Brumal florist's delight.

Déja-Vu

Let us be the seams of kisses
Within the garment of love,
Foamy dreams in the night's
Shadowy net of carp,
My Laura of laurels.

Clouds copulate
In trousers of stars.
Silent affair of the portico,
The road peppered
With milk-cartons, green colts.

Two women dreamed they were
Carousels, mares entwined.
Conjoined song rises from insomnia
And Lachesis' scissors.

Love is two obscurities
Devoured a sole match,
Interrogated by the tunnel of lies.

My soul is a rollercoaster
Barefoot in oily portals to wards.
Abstinent flesh infiltrated by sunray, stamen, sting.
Unleavened phantoms make love in the Ferris
wheel.
The circles of arms spin oblivion into jars,
Cut hearts into rivers of song

Your eyes are but tormented manors,
Aching rails.
Destiny breaks loose on jasmine, spindles, needles.

I'm a thimble, a thorn,
You are a star.

Lust is a stereo, sedates pinwheels
Seduces pines of drunkenness.
Love is but an envious gramophone
Half comatose, ashen lips
She goes crazy without the amusement or climax,
Hangs herself in the gallows of her tresses
With a pamphlet to Venus's carillons.

Transients of shadows in amorphous trains
Destined to some Wonderland
Neglected the world in sepia
Each child bloodied,
Throttled with coming of age
Ligatures of foreskins, tassels
Final gasp of a blood-clod
Kneeled, praised clemency
To the nun of cigarettes,
The thirteenth streetlamp,
Thistle-clad.

Wild

The earth sleeps like a poor sunny-faced child.
In the deep flesh of the jungle,
Forbidden fruit hangs high.

Trees steal the stars' passions.
Sea assaults sky,
Darkness covers the vagrant soul.

The spider laces her dream weaver.
The sick miner rests under my forlorn branches.
His heart pricked by the fecund rose

The night is dark, and stars fall to the earth.
The eyes of lust are green,
He wears gray shadows to cover orange fiery rage.

A panther hungry for youth, for freedom, flesh,
Searches like a brumal dream for insomniacs.
A river looks for a rose.

Anonymous Severing

I. I would ensconce my eyes
To exist in padlocked souls.

II. Her womb only bore shadows,
She was a carousel in a sea of rollercoasters.

III. Quartz moon coalesces
Into a crystal ball of shadowy séances.

IV. Butterflies morph into syringes.
Bullets undulate from clandestine graves of scythes.

V. Everything is a miracle of despair;
Everything is burdened then emptied.
Great River of hoarse bells giggles between irises
and toenails.

VI. Night lashes me with its sash of smoke,
It girdles the arteries of a clotting hope.

VII. My sister weeps as if the earth is lost within a
long slumber.
Till then her roots ache,
Her heart of anchors drowns in the dead ocean.

VIII. Sing, dance and consume fleshy questions of
the sand,
Queen of pocket-watches, clockwork moon-throb

IX. My mother left for Rasputin in an overcoat of
despair.
Numbered, honeyed, Love will set her free from the
Beautiful Beast.

X. I existed in the book of brine, between indents
and margins;
Dyed from the moon's blood staining my graphite
compass.

XI. Because I dis-imagined you
Oblivion appeared in graveyards, wombs, voices.

XII. Because of abrupt storms of ivy on grade
schools
A gramophone sung in a rose vinyl sounds

XIII. When your green eyes close into nuptial
dreams
I wake into midnight alleys,
Memories reel, penetrate abstinent skin.

XIV. As you begin to dream
I rise in misery.

XV. So aloof that reciprocity died on Sunday,
Anguish's waves engulfed the world's lighthouse
and our hearts.

XVI. My soul is a belfry, assaults virgin skies.
You are my eyelids, the shutters sever the sky of its
fishy nets.

Hope in Light

Hope in light,
On little boats of dream,
In stars; the flowers of the night,
On lighthouses clothed in golden suits.

From your eyes
Where the sun sets
Among your placid hills,
The fire is lit.
Our souls are merged
By the voice of spring
Amid the green avenues of pine.

Dark Light

The stars move around
The moon
As if a clock.

The stars are ghosts
In the sky
In robes
Of golden chaff
Blown across the hazy night.

The head of darkness is
The sky.
Each star is an eye.
With them I see
The despair
I weep,
I solemnly swear.

The light exists as if
It shares the stage with ghosts
In the neglected theatre
Of the abandoned city,
Where only the passionless woman
As a sea mercilessly
Pulled by moonlight
Resides in the city of shadows,
Where only the meanderer travels
Through it's empty mind.
Rooms filled with broken clocks,
Books in murdered languages
In manors with chandeliers
Scoff at him,
Ovens pile their ash,

Doors lie closed,
Windows conceal the photos of the past.

Abandoned Past
As if light
Rests on the strings of time.

In large parks
Spring weeps,
Willows grow,
Winter smiles and bluebells sprout
Past homeless houses,
Through a dark city,
Where the night is crowned,
Stars thrive.

He leaves the heartless city
Into the soulless sea.

Visions of the Night

Night puts the humble shepherd,
His flock to sleep.
The wind sings it's angelic tune.
The stars form icons.

The violets join the sleeping roses.
Tall colonnades of trees shiver
Above stars shine valiantly
On the altarpiece of the night.

The stars bathe and the moon looks at herself.
A child emerges from the motionless waters
Young as time itself.
He is the voice of spring, a soul of the land.

A Dissertation of Despair

Night, but a husk-cygnet
That swam
Into alabaster despondencies,
That sank into the taciturn
Suffered of ivy,
Leafless prodigal wombs
Of linens, river of hides,
Bloodied carnations
Where death lurked as a lark
Of a deck hewn with anarchistic cards
With the hope of a submerged swimmer
In the river Styx.
Impalpable caskets aroused
Undressed logs of earth's tendons,
Disentangled from autumnal aromas.

Are we but two circles:
One of seabirds, stamens,
One of scythes, chaff.
Both dissolved into silver irises,
Conjoined by an overpass
Of musky vagrancies,
Pomona's nectarine pubis
Via Dolorosa of unseen,
Stairway or crucifixes of
Solitude's crossroads,
Of starless sand-specks
Upon ashen walls,
Where nature morts
With cored nooses of Nativity lights'
Hung in inert panes?

The soul's bungalow vacant,
Aching columns,
Only a glass hummingbird,
Nestled with mummified flowers
Of solitude.

In what pity does rain torment the tormented?
Who mourns the mourners?
Who dreams the dreams the last?
What extinguishes stars?

Territory of sorrow:
Of pixelated clouds, abloom geysers
Of love-letters, green sprig-pen,
Vellum of tears, enveloped
In twine, stamps of autumn-cleaved
Hills, marks of anguish's mercuric tides,
Embalmed in Hermes's
Pannier of virgin-kisses.

I shall be an anchor in
Your mesh of obscurity,
An anvil, corroded arms
Of obstructed obols,
Moored to the dollar-bill of the narcissistic sky.
Everyone is a numismatic
Schooled on mint-tea,
Omniscient eye of the monolith,
But my soul, that lacks
The cold silver of your green torso
In the heady founts of colognes.

In what melancholy do sweet words,
Rain on tormented objects,
Satiate the parched lips,

Of the brumal earth?

Die and resurrect yourself
In pistils of stars among thorny galaxies,
Dove in unfastened skies of Orion's quivers.
Impalpable amber filtered
With the sun's cigarette of moon-cores.

If I die, perhaps, again
From oblivion's clench
And rouge-smattered lies,
I would be the pen of lime
To erase the easels
Of stifling hammam-filled cities.
The vagrant ash gags and torments,
With colonnades of indigent smoke
Of an embittered caress,
Upon the fish of hope
In the river of coalescing blood.

The Haven with its diadem of incense
Galoshes of tresses,
Navel of my loneliness.
Hope's road for a throat.
The sky with the dead at its pupils.
The living - at its toenails.
The lovers on the bosom of fury.

You, her ego's lash flits
Into the minestrone
Of streetlamps.

A Sand Full of Stagnant Questions

I.
Why does the butterfly of dreams sleep on rain's
teacup?
Is love knowing or unknowing?
Why does dew torment nascent tombstones?
How can the sea sing, with so much foam in his
mouth?
Who lights up stars?

II.
Do all the coins of meteors fall through the sky's
holey jacket?
Why when the poor rain sings it reminds me of your
bluesy voice?
Is the comet's exoskeleton of ash or honey?
Where does the solemn wake of stars terminate?
How many dreams are there in a night?

III.
Are sorrows piled high like plates on the piney lands?
For whom does the road undress?
What bayoneted the fish of hope?
What if a dove entered a great clash of bloods?
Who drafts the manifesto of streetlamps?

IV.
Is there anything freer than the tulip-barge
approaching the isles of kisses?
Is the opaque night a cuckoo clock spewing silent
stars?
What is the kindling of love's fire?
Is the summit but iron's mound of wineglasses?
Who paints autumn crimson?

V.

Is the cedar indigent or is that her diadem of drunken stars?

Does the curtain obstruct the horizon and window's affair?

Am I upon the mountain of melancholy or within the chasm of dream?

Does the flower close herself to avoid the sea's prying spume-hands?

Are doors pistils of saloons?

VI.

Are the notches of my eyes snowy or flowery?

Why does undressing secrets get heavier and heavier?

Am I an unlit candle in the conflagration of humans?

Are there unities in dissensions?

Are voices the sea's entity, souls the sky's, bones the land's?

VII.

What does the firefly dream of among the blue twilights?

Is my soul a window or a door?

Do people have roots?

Do lovers have hearts?

Do stars have prickles?

VIII.

How can we tell solitude exists when she is mute?

Is money opiate, oil - liquor?

Is indulgence blind on Sundays?

What fills emptiness?

Does the fish of hope live in the net of caresses?

IX.

Is all love in vain?
Were anguish's silver waves born from the quarry of
loneliness?
Why is life so capricious?
Is laughter a byproduct of weeping?
Are shutters the eyelids of houses?

X.
Do roads live in voices or voices in roads?
What fuelled the infatuation between the streetcar and
rain?
Does hope loath lighthouses?
When I die will a cherry tree germinate from my
brow?
Do dim stars seduce Nativity-lights?

XI.
Is the arms' crucifix corroded or oxidized?
Is everything moist with oblivion?
What if spring slept in, would it remain gelid?
Is wine the prophet of grapes?
Why do sad crows alight on drunken carillons?

XII.
Did piety corrupt the cocotte?
Are serpents earth's wires, suffusing despair in
voltages of tears?
Did the hand of death strike Bethlehem?
Is my mouth full of blood or carnations, scald or
foam?
Did the wind lash the shadowy river of mares?

XIII.
Is fall's pubis of gourds?
Are embers flame's disciples?
Does chaff become stars?

Does night forge gold into comets?
When I am melancholic, is my compass allied with the falling sun?

XIV.
Does love suddenly stop in the morning?
Is that when trains rise and get filled like tribunals?
Are the flame-lips of the cigar igniting the avenue of cedars?
How does day know of the existence of stars?
Do the carcasses of moons live in eternal rivers?

XV.
Do these rivers sing to nude roses?
Did the rose's roots entwine an eviction notice?
Does night consume the cake of tall stars with icing of snow?
Are leaves the elm's tutu, gracefully swaying on the papery earth?
Did that elm become the understudy of the paper crane?

XVI.
Who loves the unloved?
Why is my soul so much like a broken shackle?
Who hears the waters of time drowning the crystal days?
Does the vagrant smoke find shelter in the hearth?
Why does dawn gag dreams?
Why does insomnia slaughter them?

The Child's Decalogue

I. Let the inner child bleed, bleed to near death and
then out will come a man, a man with lion's blood
and a mighty roar.

II. Your father is a king and your mother is a queen,
but for you their smiles are inferior to that of a
stranger's.

III. As a child I had money, courage but no
freedom, now I have no money, some courage but
an endless sea of freedom.

IV. Feel love and admire beauty, live in the
reflection of God, do not cross into His shadow with
hatred and vanity.

V. Many trees grow in clusters, warm one another,
but the one I notice shivers alone.

VI. Money, Beauty are fleeing horses, Integrity is a
dog at his master's feet.

VII. Paint on the canvas of life, the crisp red of a
first love, the ocean blue of longing. Let the sun
dance upon the painting and absorb all, all of your
passions and dreams.

VIII. You will rise up to the mountains with your
greatest moments and descend to the valleys with
your worst blunders. The wind of other's actions
and the rain of other's words will make you come

down from the mountain. You will find iron in those valleys and you will climb up, in both of these situations you will arrive onto the meadow of a merely mundane existence.

IX. Our life is built on contrasts of a beginning and an end, of love and hatred, but all of us can be united in happiness and love, can dance around the everlasting flame.

X. Accomplish all you can in the day and all that you have forgotten hides in the twilight. The forgotten soon vanishes as valiant cavaliers into the dead of the night.

Driving By

The city
Struggles,
Its citizens are lost souls,
Its buildings need to stand the test of time.
They want to leave the hate,
But life doesn't have second chances.
They are cold, grumpy, bitter,
Even the places meant to have bliss have none.

The amusement park rots away, the paint pealed.
No kids run around, smile and scream.
The toy store, doors closed.
In that pain comes a miracle for so few.
The lucky people, they say,
Sell all they can to leave,
Sacrifice now, success later.
They sell what they can,
Wave goodbye and move on
Drive last time on this path
To a new home,
To a new city,
To a new life.

Rain or Sun?

The tears of pain were sowed in her eyes
By her own mother.
A daughter's hate,
The seeds in the ground,
A place of pain and suffering,
But then the seeds come out of the ground
intertwined,
Rise higher and higher towards the sun.

They are happy now, bask in the sun.
They have not faced the harsh downpour of the rain,
Lay blissfully with other flowers.

But then the rain comes down and the door opens.
She looks into her mother's eyes.
It rains hard on them,
The pain of yesterday brought back to life.

She looks into her mother's eyes, tears,
reconciliation.
Her mother smiles and the two hug.
The hard rain turns into a drizzle before it vanishes.
It leaves a rainbow, the sun rays, the fluffy clouds.

The rain is gone, never to come back.

Mill

Between hands and lips,
Lips and hands
There are fields
Brim with yesterdays
Sprout to hourglasses.

Today goes to mill itself:
Seconds mature into hours.
The star hides her flour sack
In your hair.

We buy the future in dozens
Of days, months, years, hands.

Hunger

Wild girl of the night
Adorned in Heaven's diamonds.
Her skirt dances in the wind.
The clouds tore the sky apart

She rose like smoke from ash.
Acute eyes burned in her soul's fire.
Her coral lips sung as the wind.
I hungered like a blind man.

In Me Your Destiny

You were a clutch of eyes amidst my blind heart.
My love wrestled with the anchored hours.
Departed the land of childhood.
I was born in laughter's river,
Severed among starry garlands.

My love grows thirsty, without any bottle
To encapsulate the moon, feed rustic echoes,
Our mouths are hungry to no avail,
Veiled in my misery, flowered into kisses for
nobody.

You are nothing since I created you
Not of scald or metals, but rather aromas.
I am nothing, because you are everything:
The moonshine, the sunshine
Mother of pearl, pearl of mother,
Mother, daughter, sister,
Gardener of frost,
Queen of voices,
Nothing, everything.

I, you, the world, my emptiness fill you,
Street sweeper of dreams,
Ruler of miracles.
My heart shows you the way to
The archipelago of nostalgia,
Which originated in the sea of people,
The battlefield of kisses,
Where ringed hands
Brought silenced mouths
To drunken, daffodil morgues.

The world laughs, you weep.
The world weeps, you laugh.
The world survives, you dream
To survive inside a dream.

My dream of you,
My winged eyes
Penetrate your flower,
Rise from the sunken
Isle of my lips
Every hour, day, dream, destiny.

Singing Fountains, Rooted Trees

My Naiad, figurehead of the ship of dreams,
Great infinitesimal being,
Crowned by a ring of seabirds,
Dissolved into a sole dove
Among thorny stars.

The sea bleeds into your green eyes.
The whole world oxidizes.
Everything has roots.
Everything is a flower,
But you.

Brows: seagulls intoxicated on brine
And the sunny void.
A heart like a sky,
Where my kisses tinged, candidly as stars.
My eyes became gears,
Axles in the moon's Dream-clock.

The conch unleashes the insidious river of music
"Does love change hips or lips, lands or hands?"

Am I yours,
Are you mine?
Or are we ours?
The womb's,
The water lily's,
The wake's?
(This lingers on cerulean shells.)

The moon is a half emptied carton of milk.
Medea's blood capsized like a topaz into the grave.

The sky: a carafe of tears cascades
Over spume-laden and radiant orchids.
A portmanteau of a quiescent summit
Nefarious, motive shadows,
Recedes among resounding echoes.

Your nocturnal gaze solidifies
The barge of my iron-wrought name
Above the white river's estuary.
A sonorous hymn of fountains
Pervades the jaded earth,
Ours to dream over.

Butterflies of Dreams of Butterflies

Through snowfall, dewfall, nightfall
You are the flower that rises,
From the isle of my sunken lips,
Wounded by a wandering dream,
Adrift in the glint
Of my grey, wet eyes
As if moths seamed to the thread
Of your rose undressed
Beneath the land of spring,
Adrift in a haze,
Abandoned slowly, suddenly.

Somewhere between my silhouette
And your mouth something wailed
On the childhood road peopled
With flowering kisses
And rustic echoes.

I owned every star,
But your eyes.
The universe is yours,
But my heart is ours.
We are two moths
Bray, bankrupt of dreams
In the net of autumn,
A fall solitary,
As if a stray dog
On inhospitable tongues
Guided by the butterfly of your name:
Mariposa,
The little wings of laughter.

Soul Love

I love you like the silvery veins of the moon,
The clusters of palms in the vagrant desert.
I love you as something impalpable
That lives in the lips,
But can only be felt by the soul.

In every star lie your narrow, moist eyes.
In every ocean - your wet lips.
In every sunray - your golden locks.

Do not smile for me,
Just flutter your eyes.
Do not bring me to the full stage of June
Rather to the empty scene of October.
Do not bring me to the staleness of your lips,
But to the freshness of your soul.
I want to be an ocean,
Your little waves caress me.

The Sun is a Star.
I drew comet streaks
Across your long blazing locks,
Crowned you with burned-out stars
As the tower has its clock piece,
The day - your radiant light and burning soul
As if you were Mother Spring.
I have you as Madame Autumn
I chiseled away the moon,
Pulled you into my hands.
We danced through the stars
Like little lights that flickers
On the brim of seas.

My love, my freedom, my light
You left me to be with Father Day,
To chase Cronus around,
The beds of water and the blankets of land,
To roll on the horizon
Like a coin on pavement.

In all my rage, my failing passion, my crumbling
love,
I weep as meteors tumble
I cry as purple rain falls
I shudder - a star tumbles off the dome of the
universe
I shiver - trees lose their coats.
Soon my eyes as if far away planets,
Take one last glimpse at the river
Rusted with copper,
Above the silver veins of the moon bleed starlight.
I as the sonata of the night
Disappear in the harmony of dawn
To join the sunrise's fresco.

Here I Bade Farewell

Here I bade farewell
Leaves of love have fallen
From my soul
And our love
Runs wild
In the meadow of mundanity
In late November
Where the frost
Covers the moral compass,
Where the light is dim
Where the flame flickers.

I asked the Lord
For your tender hands
As the sweet August
That seduced us.
I asked Him
For your moist lips
As the sea of my tears
That separates our souls,
But our shadows
Waltz on the fervent waves
As if one.

I asked the Sun
To shine on
Destiny's road,
But it slept in vanity.
I asked the Stars
To radiate
The endless tears in the sky,
But the bright city lights
Murdered their passions.

I soon realized:
You were a horse
That left the July sun
To be blinded by November.
I crafted a vessel
From your soul's ice
And set you upon
The never-ending river,
Where the rain of word's
Chilled your corpse,
But the snow
As if it were a sad song
Quivered your soul.

Soon you were a sonata
In the harmony of life,
A star that shines in the day,
Sleeps in the endless night.

As I winced,
I saw the sunset framed you
As you set a kiss upon a swallow
That journeyed from soul to soul.

I pray to the Lord
For a final note
As I run into the forest,
Find the water
Your heart needs.
I moisten it with
The water of youth
Only to realize
I had journeyed to the sea of tears.

As I bathe my longing in the river
And place it into the sun's golden locks
It blackens the sun's soul.
Under the twilight
We exchange kisses.
The river takes you
Through the sea of tears.
As the boat melts
Our love plunges
Into the sea
Of corpses.

It is only in the eternal sun
Do I meet a hand so tender.
Lips so moist,
Fire so warm.

Post-Mortem

I.
Between dreams and cots
Abstinent from warehouses
In the boudoirs of virgins
And my windowless soul
Love spread itself in garlands of clouds,
Clandestine hazels
Among your laky eyes that
Grasped shadowy minnows,
Moored to the sky of my brow.
Solitude's pincered
As if drunken bells
Of emancipated doves.
A raven exasperated,
A bee among the moon's stamens
Whitened your diurnal hills of eulogies.

II.
I, resurrected like a lighthouse
Doused of hopes
With your subdued prophecy
Of aged mirrors, neon sermons.
Nascent swarms of scythes severed me
Into cologne-anchors of snuff-bottles
That, furious waitresses vend to narcissistic queens
And their dead infinities of regattas:
Oars of imperceptible hearts,
Oblivion, but riggered in spumy reveries
Rose from a slumber of substance
With a cascade of hope,
That snowed onto my barren soul

In the form of wheat-ears,
Weeping violets
Flasks of sorrows, lesions.

III.
Death: a kiln of ash, wombs
In streams of Christmas lights
That exonerated my chaste soul
Of inky armoires, milky chrysalises
Among aromas of a lonely
Wharf where the barge of kisses,
Keeled of enigmatic mouths,
Within waters of time,
Departed for your isle rooted
In my laughter
That was the offshoot
Of your melancholy
Forged of aloofness,
Upon this carousel-world,
Where our lives infused tears
As wicks or roads
Of matted, snaky coils,
Ensconced bread's
Breasts of chaff
Solitude promulgated:
Guitars of crows,
Chords of mourning.

Paradise/Paraíso

The light hits the sleepy sky.
The road snakes.
The stars lash
As Christmas lights.
The moon bleeds silver.
Pure woman of the Moon
We walk in love,
Hand in hand
For in you all is born.
They sleep in my soul.
Nothing has a name:
Leather, Fire, Iron,
But they live in you.
I do not live in the canyon of your marble legs.
I do not live in your forests of thoughts.
I live in your blood,
In the valley of your heart.
That night the horizon paints small ships,
So I row for your gift:
The rings of Saturn.

Paradise/Paraíso (Spanish)

La luz golpea el cielo adormecido
El camino se serpentea
Las estrellas se destellan
Como las luces de Navidad
La luna sangra de la plata
Mujer pura de la Luna
Caminamos en amor,
Mano en mano
En tú, todos son nacidos,
En mi alma ellos duermen
Nada tienen un nombre,
Piel, Fuego, Hierro
Pero, ellos viven en ti
No vivo en el cañón de tus piernas de mármol
No vivo en tus bosques de ideas
Vivo, en tu sangre,
En el valle de tu corazón
Y esa noche el horizonte, pinta pequeñas naves
Eso, yo remo por tu regalo:
Los anillos del Saturno

We are all Kings and Queens

You reign in the
Depths of my heart.

I drown
In the river of voices.

Beyond the bed
Second-hand dreams are refunded.

I hitchhike your hips
In my name's overcoat.

Everybody goes, reaps memories
On the road to their happiness.

You rain in the
Depths of my heart.

Two Lips, One Heart

One winter night
The vagrant stars danced to please
The moon's glow.
She laid on the hostile pavement
Asleep as the snow brought forth a coat,
As if it had swallowed the whole moon.
The moonbeams danced from her soul
Through her skin to moon's shadow.

I tried to soothe her body
To feel what a first kiss was
As if our lips were one,
To fill her mind
With African Sands,
The Wild West,
To feel her soul.
I had to be daring, bold
As the winter may
Have left her to sleep in eternity,
Run far from town
Into the foothills.

The flowers were asleep, bulbs closed.
I took the nearest one,
Nestled it in her locks.
I dove in the deepest ocean,
Stole the oyster's greatest treasure,
Positioned the pearl upon her tongue.
I entered the tallest tower,
Climbed to the summit,
Where I plucked one of the stars
Placed it in her palm.

In the cold I too fell asleep

In the morning
Our eyes met.
Her hair radiated
As the rays of the sun.
The flowers had opened its petals
As if the were the centre of the soul.
The star had turned to a diamond
Which shimmered upon her finger.
The pearl had dissolved on her tongue
She began to stammer and soon speak.
Her first words expressed her longing to dance.

I opened my arms and my heart.
We danced to our heartbeat,
To the sun's glow
Through the day.
The Ogre of winter's heart of ice
Fell onto the pavement,
Shattered into pieces
The ice retreated
The water carried him far from here.

The awoken maiden of spring,
He danced with her
So passionately, so vividly
As time lingered on.

A Soul is a Sea

I wore a coat of lily pads
Over me her words, her last words rained.
So hard they poured until a little sparrow
Of hope signaled and doves flew through the air.

She buried our flame
In the cemetery of broken loves.
Made our path untraversable.
The windows where we declared our love
No longer lived.

My body grew larger,
My mind - stranger
But my soul was still
As a sea on the dawn of spring.

Her soul was black and feathered.
She flew away from me in the midst of the night.
With the sunrise a lotus bloomed,
The aroma filled the senses with a new beginning.

Your soul melted on the seaside
Waves brought the sand and the remains
Into the sea, my sea.

I searched for pearls
Love, happiness were little gems
In the far stretches of Neptune's realm.

I searched for many moments:
Your stashed kisses from me in seashells
I hid secrets in bubbles.

Many waves pass
I look for those miracles,
Mirages danced in African sands.

My sea tarnished
With the blood of unfaithfulness
Became the sea of blood.

Our love dissipated as sea foam
Over the ocean of eternal longing.
The lasting thoughts
Disappeared in the winter wind.

A Horizon of Love and a Sea of Dreams

You are a little star I dance to.
For me you are the jewel of every-night.
Someone loves the sunset, another – the moon,
But I love you.

Our love is as enduring as the soul
As objects that don't open the eyes or stimulate our minds.
Love is not the brother of lust,
Love is summer surrounded by winter frost.

You are a fruit that never lost its sweetness,
The scent of an evergreen that never fades,
A ship that never docked.

You are a flower.
You live for one hundred nights.
On the one hundredth instead of losing beauty
You disappear in the wind, a violet amidst roses,
But do not worry I love violets.

Your eyes can't open,
Your hands can't feel.
But do not worry this makes you closer to the things,
Which matter most.

You made a home for us that lasted eternity.
A home that I could love, live and dream about.
Offered endless fire of love, and water of life.

You were the sun and I was the forest,
You offered me endless love,

But the trees withered.
New trees needed to grow
For the love to live on.

You were the sky and I was the land
We met over the eternal horizon.

Raining Time and Bleeding Love

The sun withers, the moon grows.
A day fights another, but a night bows to the next.
Look into the night sky, find the vibrant stars.
The brightest star dances within.

Let my mind, my body to feel age, seasons,
Let sparrows perch in my soul,
Let children polka to my heart beat forever.

Sow seeds of love in our minds,
Teach us what love, man of piety, of grace are.
Let these roses never lose colour,
Never fade from our paradise of desires.

Flowers of love, never of lust
They long water and sunshine
Love brings water to the soul,
Lust brings wine to our mind
Love brings souls together,
Lust – a body atop another
Love warms the heart,
Lust incites the eyes
Love is of eternity,
Lust lasts a moment.

One hundred kisses may leave nothing more than a
stain.
A smile of an instant can last half a century.

Swim in the rivers of life.
Bask in the sun of youth.
Climb many summits,

Cross many paths
Dance, my dearest.
Grow, my strongest.
Feel to the fullest, my wisest
Dance in colour, with violet and pink until
The sun of youth is covered by clouds,
The thoughts, the actions of adults rain over your
head
To ravage the only world those eyes have ever
witnessed.

A Clock in Paradise

Take a breath,
Close your eyes
And enter
Past Lilly cups, daffodils.

I have waited so long next to melted clocks
Dreams wither so quickly,
But showers save a withering rose

Do not wade away,
Do not sail away
My dear never to freeze,
My flame is here.

Rest in my meadows
Ride my rivers and roads
Find warmth in my sun's glow.
Light a flame in the night,
Feel my presence,
Smell my roses
Taste my golden apples.

Spend Eternity here.
Love will never wither,
Never from your thoughts,
Never you away from me.

You are a castaway
Without age,
Rich of my gifts
But what makes you long are

The elms and the violets across the bay,
The warmer sun and lighter clouds

I wanted to be the sparrow,
You to become spring.
But spring leaves the sparrow
As you leave my isle to another.

Everyday I see you - I wither
Until I am frail and barren.
One day you long for me and sail across.
I am cold and shiver among the stars.

Wilted Roses and Shaking Stars

There they sat
Dear children of love,
Silent but passionate,
Forbidden but free.
Like the way rain nourishes the grass
Their love began as a drizzle,
Metamorphosed into a storm inside their hearts,
A united flame.

Her garden was a home to their love.
In the night they became one.
A midsummer's night
Surrounded by roses and flames
Protected them
From the soldiers.

Their love had no condition,
But to the soldiers
Love was alien
They counted the bills,
Their only preoccupation,
On the top of the pyramid of power.
These children held out for so long
So pure, so beautiful, so young, so pious
But the soldiers entered one day.

The night can only stay so long.
The summer only so much longer.
The roses wilted and colour left them.
The flame burned out.
It was time that fought with love.
They looked to each as they were dragged away,-
A time when love was misunderstood.

Here I walk, a wanderer without hope.
Their love was anachronistic,
A little piece of heaven in hell.
A love bound by hearts,
Not by lips
Or deep pockets
In another time.
A love such as theirs will unfold,
But our eyes may never catch a glimpse.

Come, my dearest
Through their garden,
Pull the sun over the moon,
Plant roses,
Bring back Mother Spring
. And light their flame.

Look above:
You will see two stars shiver
As if a fire burns between them.

Two Monologues (Drama)

I.

My heart's want for your love fills the empty night.
The night brings me marigolds to pin to my aching heart.
I imagine walking through purple mountains and crystal skies
Guided by my soul's compass
Where you shall dance freely in the wind.
The wind who will loosen her hand from mine
Sail me to your wide arms
Stretched from zenith to star of my suffering.
Light travels barefoot through the night
To rest on your soul.
My heart will fly through the heavens
In the cordillera sun,
Search the rustle of the elms that shelter you
Flee from the net of darkness,
Subdued by starlight,
Dyed by the oranges of autumn.

II.

The love letter dances above the fire.
Stars fall into earth's poor hands.
Green smoke fills the vagrant night.
The sea embraced the sky.
The bramble holds the oak.
Only we hunger for love.
You are away from my world.
I shall rest like a child
Under the bramble tree.
The vain night hides you,
But I shall wait like a lamppost for your star
To shine on my soul.

I shall search through the rivers, the pages.
The roses undress above the water
Here, in the sky the gulls of your brows flew.
Woman of burning passion,
Hands full of stars and seawater,
Your body was a boat that fled me,
But your heart stayed in my hands.
If only the Lord would hear my suffering
If only He saw your diamond eyes
Thirsty for my soul's water.
My longing is otherworldly,
But do not fret, our fire, our love was always first.
In the twilight where memories like thieves haunt
me
Where final dreams beg
Where love leaves unnoticed
As a farm-child running away in the night
I stay.

Andromeda or Ophelia?

I long for her eyes,
Which kindle of my unkempt existence.
You rained wounded poppies
To last the eternity of a caress,
But the moist nets of desire
Encapsulated my bony diadems
Padlocked souls, destined pallor,
Sleepy aroma of kisses that
Encircled shadowy trains
In underpasses acquainted to my heart.
Undressed mirrors envy ashen windows,
Where death lurks as if a switchman
And oblivion in stubs of aged voyages
Let me imagine the earth
Before it germinated roots
With drowned swimmer arms,
Us before we were entwined.
Bliss before it bore you,
Daughter of hope,
Conductor of autumnal violas
Switchboard operator for spring's wakeup call.
Here I love you between
Abrupt bursts of ivy and fiery graveyards.

Love is brawling lightning
Dissolve into a drop of transparent honey
Thorny stars unleash insomnia's fragrance.
I and you converge into we,
Half bloody, half empty, half dead.

Remember Magdalene?
The day consumed her in entirety,
With its pincers of haste,

Numbered and ticketed her 227 names
As if butterflies flee chrysalises of beds.
Once, errant pupae of condoms weaned on
conscience.
Death paces in telephone coils, windowpanes,
wombs
And birth in those same hushed objects

Acrobat of matches upon the chaotic trapeze
As if a pendulum lurches toward
Balconies of sorrows and their dove overcoats,
Tightropes of headstones and tresses.
I, a scarecrow decommissioned by twilight
In the sea of sirens and cherubs,
Armrests subdued by limelight
Bosom of bullets, sheepish grin.
In my palm Mary's orange rind
Traverses a sky of inkwells, Christmas lights
Milk cartons, felt storks, Zyklon pendants.

Tell me, it's blue, and starry, and nude:
Her voice and your womb.
Tell me, it's grotesque outside,
But deep inside and beautiful
Like a set of eyes or an octet of pawns,
A dozen sextants or a vastness of elm,
Or a solitary serendipity in brothels of needles,
Or my sister fills another tulip
And, perhaps, our silhouettes on silkscreens
Among the vagueness of July twenty eighth
Potts the dollar store's roses
In jars that brim with inaccessible crumbs
Of time on her platter along
With peace, war, oceans of cherries,
And the fish of hope.

Love and Lust

Our wires have been tweaked and twisted
To put lust over love.

In dingy homes, foggy skies
Do we play with lust
Alone or with another?

Lust is so often practiced,
But love universally suppressed.

Lust is readily available,
A star in the countryside,
But love is rare,
Polaris shivering alone amid city lights.

Lust is a faction of our mind,
Readily available, carnations at a florist.
We window watch
After some time in bed
Wasted by dangerous obsessions.

Through the window we see
Our families, friends, and acquaintances,
The unknown belongs in cities.

We were brave and cowardly,
Blissful and morose,
Fearless and fearful

We were like city dwellers,
As all our brothers and sisters
Except we appear beautiful,
But inside is nothing but hatred.

Outside the village we see horses
White as mother's milk,
The milk of kindness.

They travel through verdant valleys,
Snow capped peaks,
Our homes, shops, gardens.
At dusk they arrive here
Bound by lust.

Two board a horse.
Travel west from Aurea.
The day bows to night's realm.
We begin to experience something
Never felt in our hearts,
Like the first snowfall.

Lovers rule the night
Not bound by society,
Free, wild.

A Fire in Rain

It was spring when you crossed my threshold.
In our spring
You weaved me garlands of kisses
And I lit flames of lust.
Your eyes brought me to your isle.
I felt your warm curved hips
And cool narrow legs.
I stroked the deer next to them,
I smelled the rose between your breasts
And embraced you.

Summer came and went.
We waded in the river,
Friends at day
Crazed animals at night.
It was our night, for us, lovers
Walk free, walk long.
The autumn chill entered your heart.
I lifted the anchor,
But your smile brought me back.

I climbed the highest peak in the name of love.
I screamed to you at the zenith.
You ran up, a panther and a deer.
With the sunrise a passion unfolded,
But by sunset we were unknowns.

Several weeks went by in the spell,
But the winter storm chased the autumn out
And lit out the fire in the pit.
I called out to you in the vast expanse.
Where were you when I needed you most?

Were you in his arms, lips in lock?
I was true, but life gets the better of us all.

I tossed her robes onto our bed,
Hoped we can once again be together.
With time I put those thoughts to sleep,
Climbed into our bed for eternal rest.

Over There

I thought I loved you.
I crossed the seven seas
Just to see you.

I thought I wanted you.
I thought I needed you.

I thought my heart lies with you,
But my heart lies over the Pond.

Not on the lit up streets of New York,
Not on the Hollywood walk of Fame.
It lies with my family:
From the dust under the piano,
From the elms in the yard,
From the smiles of my parents
In that small country mansion.

I thought I wanted you.
I thought I needed you.

I thought my heart was with you,
But my heart lies over the Pond.

I saw you.
I thought your eyes were diamonds,
But they didn't shimmer.
I thought you would hug me once
But you never did
I thought you would look at me
Not my wallet.

I thought my heart was with you,
But my heart lies over the Pond.

You lured me
Onto that steamer of sorrow
Into those dim lit city streets.
I thought you would love my heart
Not my wallet
You never loved me.
Never kissed me.
Never looked at me.
When I started singing the Hometown blues
You shed no tears.
You couldn't care less.

I thought my heart was with you,
But my heart lies over the Pond.

You lured me like Medusa
Where to
I thought I wanted you.
I thought I needed you.
I thought love and money were different -
I was wrong.

I thought my heart was with you,
But my heart lies over the Pond.

Night Vision

The stars shake
The dim blue sky.
The moon's magic illuminates
Endless realm of night.
The sea of tears,
The cries of the wind
Chill his soul

He remembers her voice,
Her golden locks of hair ,
Wide curvy hips
Sink in the sea

He reached for her
But her road was at the end.
Her corpse lied
In the depths of Neptune's realm
She shivered with the others in the sky.

He is distraught.
This move of love
Never to be forgotten
In the game of life.

He calls to her "Aurora, Aurora, my dearest,
You and only you,
The only breasts I'll ever touch so gently,
The only hand I'll ever hold so tenderly,
The only soul that will light an inextinguishable
flame".

He hears the echo of her voice
He swims to her. The night sky has another star.

Union (II)

I search for the burning fragrance of the rose
Under the curtains of the sky,
Above the roofs of forests
For your spring-like voice
For your mother like hand.

I love my eyes for they saw you
I love my arms for they felt you.
I love my soul for it understood you.

Love is a rose
Seen only by the eyes of the soul.
Lust feeds the eyes,
But love is a song of the soul

Love is red as the passion of blood.
Love is a wine that trickles into the mouth,
That spreads like a rage.
Love is a silken robe,
White as a child's conscience
Floats on the water's of life.
Love is a dreamy star in the skies of reality.
A breath in our lives.

I was young in your arms.
An inferno blazed in my heart.
My lonely soul grew sickly
Without yours.

For these moments of love, grow roses
That lift us from the simple earthy hands
To join stars, the soul of the skies

In these cool autumn nights
We found love and lost love
Until two distant stars
Were born into the sun

Purgatory/El Purgatorio

I still dream of your body
As a snowy mountain clothed
In marigolds of tenderness.
The river of secrets shines like silver,
Roses undress between your breasts.
I walk in my robe with tears
In your dream world,
The world of peace, doves
The land of hope, bells.
Do not bring me lilies from the edge of the ocean.
Do not bring me water from the mountains.
Night falls on my soul and I live,
Live with the pale image of you
Among the jungle of my chaos.
Between are your arms that open and close
Stolen by a sordid Spanish.
The villages of my soul
Fall into the hand of death,
That lifts them to an impenetrable cloud castle
Without hope, without you.
But one day you will come, queen of the moon,
With your mother of pearl wings
And we will rest on the moon
Until,
Time separates my soul
In a cemetery of glass
And the sun shines on you, in vain.

Purgatory/El Purgatorio (Spanish)

Sigo soñar sobre tu cuerpo
Como, una montaña nevada vestía
En las caléndulas, de la ternura.
El río de los secretos brilla como plata,
Las rosas se desnudan entre tus pechos.
Yo camino, en mi bata de lágrimas
En tu mundo de ensueño.
El mundo de paz, de palomas
La tierra de esperanza, de campanillas
No trae a mí, los lirios del borde del océano
No trae a mí, el agua de las montañas
La noche cae en mi alma y yo vivo,
Vivo con la imagen pálida de ti
Entre la jungla de mi caos
Entre, son tus brazos eso abren y cierran
Robado por un español sórdido
Las aldeas de mi alma,
Caen en la mano de la muerte
Que los levanta les a un castillo impenetrable de
nubes
Sin la Esperanza, sin ti
Pero, un día tu vendré, reina de la luna
Con tus alas de madreperla
E iremos a descansar en la luna
Hasta que,
Tiempo separa mi alma
En un cementerio, del vidrio
Y el sol ilumina tú, en vano

Love in the Water/Amour dans les Eaux

Your water, your words, phrases nourish my life
worn roots.
The fire of passion burns my wooden soul.
In your eyes there is a sea of colors,
Azure oceans, turquoise forests, fuchsia skies.

I am infatuated by the scent of your soul.
When the little star that brought our hands together
Burns through the night
Your smile, a little vessel sails through the lakes of
my tears
And brings me to the leafy isles of your soul.

The tides rise to the moons and misery rained upon
me.
Cold by neglect, rise through the waters
Past the mountains of your breasts,
The rough-cut diamonds of your eyes
For the star of your soul.

Love in the Water/Amour dans les Eaux (French)

Votre eau, vos mots, vos phrases nourri mes racines
portées par la vie
Le feu de la passion brûle mon âme de bois
Dans tes yeux il y a une mer de couleurs,
Des Mers azur
Des forêts sarcelle
Un ciel fuchsia
Je suis entiché
Par l'odeur de votre âme

Quand la petite étoile a amené nos mains
Brûle dans la nuit
Votre sourire, est un petit navire qui navigue à
travers les lacs de mes larmes
Et m'amène aux îles arborées de votre âme
Les marées montent à la lune et la misère pleut sur
moi
Froide par la négligence, je me lève des eaux froides
Je passe les montagnes de vos seins, les diamants de
vos yeux
Pour l'étoile de votre âme

A Seeking

I searched for you through the skies of my dreams,
The lakes of tears
The forests of my thoughts,
My roots sought an alien land
My star - a new sky.
Searched for lips and found a soul.
Wanted fire and drunk water.

In these brumal times
Your green sheltered me
My seamstress, you knit my dreams
My flower girl, brought blue, ethereal flowers,
Garlands of kisses

Her arms destined to my lands with oils and
fragrances
Of oranges and roses.
Her hands: little butterflies,
Orange and paper-like,
The silver of her smile,
The green of her eyes as the forest,
Where the barriers to our love fell like trees,
Where lighting stroke like the insanity of love
Where the fire burnt, one night and one only.

Her dress was not long
Violet, deathlike,
Yellow as bees, gold, stars, sunflowers,
Long and straight.
Nature's warrior
Stretched to the sun itself
To you, luminous and desirable
Here in the skies and pines

We danced and embraced.
Felt as the world's great plates to each other's mercies
Villages ravaged except for the gingerbread town hall
Towns abandoned except for grandiose vessels
Great cities lay ruined except for silver churches
Nations far and wide desolate except for the dream factory,

Butterflies in transparent cases, ivy like secrets in the walls,
Yet in these winters came springs greater and fuller.
The gingerbread lost taste to rich cream.
Flight came and left.
The spire glowed golden.
The ivy grew like obelisks.
The butterflies carried the dreams far and wide
But found one another once
Like a child finds a mother
Like a star - the sky
When lost once.

He consumed the desert sand
Oblivious to his coat of embraces
Wore his garment of tears.
The vagabond searched
As the dried river for the sea
Before night hushed the earth with winter,
Broke dreams like glass,
Tucked him into the earth as a mother,
But he rose like a butterfly,
His soul, empty and solitary.

Empty Road

When my hand felt yours,
It was the union of earth and sky.
When the earth slept,
The snow fell in a thousand arrows,
My hand hid itself in your hair's nest.

You etched on my body as if a canvas.
I find myself in you like a sea.
I want to caress the way the night caresses a star.

Love you like a child loves summer,
So intoxicated with roses,
Afraid of dust and lime
I search for your silver footsteps,
Golden hair strewn
Across the forest floor.

Nameless

The desert, long and unending as a serpent
Peopled with circus troupes and Gypsies.
I too am forgotten, without a name, a home.

The wind sings your name,
The stars dance in the arms of the night.

The moon is full of light and I of loneliness.
Above the sky you wait in a sea of resting stars.

The moon is your heart,
Comets your long stringy hair

The stars one by one depart on a train of shadows
And I imagine I am the ruler of the desert,
Stepping on a sand tower to embrace you

As if I was the tide rising to the moon

Castle in the Sky

The birds follow the distant tune of your song.
When I exclaim your name the stars, as if lamps,
Bring light to the avenues of the sky.

On this solemn night I speak every word and phrase,
"Your eyes are diamonds,
I want you as the earth longs for April."
Love never crosses the threshold of my lips.

Love belongs to the soul.
Why am I alone
When you are not in my arms?

The night is dark and solemn.
The magician has hidden all the light.
The stars fall into deep slumber.
The sun no longer let the moon to continue her
fraud.

I am dressed in your embraces,
Satiated by your sonnets,
I wait on a bed of sand.
The night grew antsy and fled on a boat of violets.
Light broke through the pines as a rabble of
butterflies,
Rose me to her Castle in the Sky.

Sleeping Heart

The diamond stars shine fervently.
The night dresses the naked roses in dark robes.
She places her joy in the azure seas, in a casket of
flowers
Her tears cover his snow face from the sun's glow.
She places the rose of her fire onto the plains of his
heart.

The wind hushes him into a sombre slumber.
The moonlight strikes through the tears
Like a hand through black hole.
A stork falls from the never-ending sky,
Leaves him rest alone on the rings of Saturn
Under a cemetery of stars,
Under the roar of a silently wild night.

Departed Love

The gulls of your brows drunken with salt and
passion
Fly into the never-ending sky.
The vessels of your smiles thick with oils
Cruise into the incessant seas.
Your diamond eyes fall into the waters.
Your golden sun-rays from sky to sea.
Soon there comes a point
When I must let the struggling bird free.

You intoxicated with freedom, chase day's justice.
You part the circle of my arms,
The rim of my world.
The flowers of love wilt without your soul-water.
As a starless sky I wait.
My soul chilled by winter,
My eyes dimmed by darkness
Stay motionless in the eve of your departure.

These great lands fall asleep
With the opiate of unrequited love.

Died with the Wind

She came and went like spring,
Lighted up the villages in my soul.
Angels were born from the darkness of chasms.
Infants in still waters were death bathed.
She was covered in winter's tears.
She rose, that child of love,
To become woman of passion.

Her passion outgrew her.
She died because she could no longer love.
She didn't have the key to enter the city of life.
The eyes of my soul
Became obsolete in the infinite darkness.
My lands chilled by winter
Fell into deep sleep.

Sonnet of Longing (I)

I search for you in abandoned theatres,
In the rivers of sweet sublime sounds,
Daughter of infinite passion, of unending love.

Death was the train that traversed.
The time riddled paths of your soul.
You were the star that warmed glacial lakes, bitter
hands.
You were the light that guided souls into the skies.
Darkness filled your soul.

To motherless children you lowered your tender
hands.
In the climax of winter you sing of sweet spring.
I lift you from the hard, poverty stricken face of the
earth
Into the otherworldly skies
To shine valiantly like a cross on the slender altar of
the night.

Sonnet of Longing (II)

The wind with its tunes from the villages in valley
depths
Hushed him to sleep on beds of bleeding geraniums.
Moonlight blanketed his shawls and soul
On paths gracefully lit by comets.

Tall shadows and lost children walked
The stars shone valiantly as if crosses
On the altarpiece of the night,
All of them shone on him.

In the dreams of all the crestfallen children
He rose to the summit
In search of the angelic voice
That guided him through the realm of the night.

As the darkness fell to his soul
It was, as if her kisses caressed his cheeks.
Through deep forests haunted by forgotten wishes,
He trudged with every footstep.

Her voice grew more vivid and full of life,
The voice of a mother's longing.

Sonnet of the Night

The artist paints all the leaves on trees green once
again.
The flowers of hope wither in abandoned fields.
The wind brings tunes from faraway mountain
villages.
Day performs her last notes, summer writes his last
stanzas.

From the moist lips of the night stars fall
Into the river's mouth turning it brilliant gold.
Tall shadows lurk over empty forest paths.
Reflections sleep on the brink of seas.
The rain of oblivion plunges in her soul,
Splits their hands from one another.

The trees carry me into the never-ending sky,
From their tips I see the pious moon
The night's wings guide me through the silence
To the unearthly song sung from a distant summit.

Winter

The sky weeps in the form of echoing gramophones:
Vinyl of rustic poppies, bluesy-rain tune, carillon-
static.
That night whitens street sweepers; salts
confectionaries.
I mediate in drowned swimmer-arms of fires,
Rosy wines of tree-trunks, hosiery of stained glass.
I loved you and you loved me more, in the verdant
desert!

You are the sole habitant on my isle of caresses.
Your eyes, lakes encircle me with a sleepy aroma of
gulls.
This whole world becomes alien again.
My longing, no longer mortal, but I am still rooted
To underbellies of insomniac, twilight-hushed cities
River of suffering empties into the ocean of the
dead.

I loved you, still: sublime, shivering star.

Autumn

You clench the flower
My brumal heart yearns for,
Dove of warring-eyes,
Bread: nourishes groins,
Heaping nectarines seize
The windowsills of your mouth with fervor,
Merger of fury and melancholy.

Oh, awning of pities, flowering avenues
With barefoot bicycles, a nude Cadillac
Smoke's sash girdles the reverberating lamppost
Heaving voices, curdling tongues
Moon fastened to obituaries
Fleeting world in which we are but timetables;
Shadowy trains vacates the luminous soul.

Summer

Here, upon coils transfusing despair,
We alighted: pigeons in dusk, pigeons over dawn,
Entombed within golden steeples
Amid the spread of days,
Emerged upon the cloud-napery.
Mountaintop wicks, sorrows for bowls, hands for
hands
Odor of nostalgia infused.

From waking and slumbers
Among daydreams of spindles and thyme
I called you Andromeda with infinite-crystal
tenderness
Anguish's waves liquidated your sweetness as if a
port.
You were in everything, filled everything:
Torn hearts, lovemaking dewdrops, ivy-sufferings.
I called you maniacal, Maria, Mary, mine.

Spring

Your mouth recalls a little vessel of hyacinths.
Fissured by simple rings, entwined in dreamy foam-
I caress you fearlessly, your sad form of tallows,
chrysalises
Among my shipwrecked heart.
Throbbing as an aged atlas or undressing roses
You are my sole lighthouse, hope's daughter,
Instantaneous kindling of love's inferno.
Net of kisses, where my fish of solitude sang.

O, frayed sand bosom, cupolas of cerulean shells,
Vagrant birds peck at thorny stars.
A wave, slightly hoarse on the briny flag
Of my maritime territory with polders, brikes
Your mouth infiltrates my ironless heart,
Weavers with desire pincers of love's mantle.

Before and After

There he was, in that school, an aquarium
There he was singing the blues,
Not a fish like the rest,
But a bird, who couldn't fly,
Forced to swim with the fish.
Alone on his on isle, marooned by the jet-set
The water so clear, of his tears.

Nobody to speak to,
Nobody to share his velvet voice,
So he writes in his journal
About his miseries, hopes, dreams, fantasies
But about reality too.

He is alone on his bed of sand until
Comes a young maiden, Mary.
The two talk on the field
He tells her what would be his final work
About thistles and flowers in the blacksmith's yard.

He continues to tell her his story
Until she cries, bangs her head on the ground.
He explains that she stained her white dress
She then puts on him a crown of thistles.
She calls him true and pure.

They continue the short lived romance
Until a gang of older boys comes.
They attack him, rip his journal.
Mary tries to help, but one of them holds her down
They beat him till his last breath.

They leave, she cries for help.

She looks frantically,
But the cards were dealt,: his path on earth is over
Mary runs to him.
She weeps over his dead body
She begins piecing the journal back,
Story by story.
She brings them to a publisher,
A book is born.

Misunderstood in life,
Revered after life.

A New Day

I thought this place of injustice was to become just.
A city of equality,
Where we would all smile, hold hands.
A city, where poor and rich would not exist.

But alas, I was wrong.
Here I am shiver,
Look down onto the city.
It is not a court, but a playground.
The injustice makes justice,
Rules the playground, the city.

They own the city,
Richer and corrupter by the day.
Walk in black suits up to their condos.
Lye nude on Copacabana and Ipanema,
But we never get to live that fantasy.

We look atop high peaks,
Watch the injustice creep like a road slithers to the
mountains,
Watch it spread like cancer

They push us further and further up the peak
Our shacks razed, condos built,
Their voice is of a man, a well-spoken man
But ours is of an introverted child, struggles to
communicate,
But he tries, he writes.
He is me, I am him.

Writes on paper
About the injustice, about poverty but about hope,

too.
Then comes the moon.
I leave my sheet to finish tomorrow

We lose everyday
But we still fight,
Shove and push our way up,
Up those crystal stairs to a glass ceiling.

Alley Cats

Alley Cats we are,
Dirty ones at best,
Prowl through the alleys,
Like misfits walk head down
In the school corridors.

La-bababadi, doubaduba di!

We scratch and fight the purebreds
We are mutts, always lose,
But so do the misfits.

Tsh-fish-fish-lish-wish!

We try our best to reach the garbage can.
We are the attention seekers,
But we always fail.
We are left with no such food.
Meow.

We, cats need our food
Like misfits need attention,
But we like them fail
Failure, inevitable.

We try our best to reach to the top
But they always push us down.
They also try to speak up
But they are shut up by the jet-sets.
We are both misfits,
Except we are just alley cats.

Prowl through the streets for the prey,
We search for a free voice,
One that isn't abashed by anyone.

Babadibababadi,
Ma ma ma ma babadi

We, alley cats belong nowhere,
But we try
To show the rulers,
Push ever so hard,
Fail every time,
But misfits don't try
They keep shut,
They MUST SPEAK UP!

We, cats need our food
Like misfits need attention,
But we like them fail
Failure, inevitable.

When one fails
Try, try, try again.

We push and shove
Vie for a piece of the prey,
But misfits keep their lips shut.

We, cats need our food
Like misfits need attention,
But we like them fail,
Failure, inevitable.

We go hungry all those nights,
Our stomachs grumble.

Misfits go silent,
Silent for months
But then they like us become restless.

We push and shove the white purebreds
And so do misfits,
They speak, speak up.
They talk, and talk.
They smile and shake hands.

We cats need our food
Like misfits need attention.
We like them try and fail,
But in the end succeed.

The Flame from Within

I was a golden man, rich yet naïve.
Money flowed out of pockets
Yet I was estranged.
From my Grandma's words of wisdom,
My son's cheery laughs and her,
The one with a glint on the fourth finger,
The one, who was the greatest mistake of my life,
The grandiose home along with wallpaper and
sycamore panels,
The lustrous crystals of my chandelier.

And then it hit.
My son strapped in his wings
Flew over the horizon, the horizon of my world, our
world.
When the wax of our connection melted
He fell down to the land of common folk,
A land of misfits, of misers and a land of meek,
Into the ocean.
He swam to the light only to know it burned out.
I remembered the day, the last sparkle in his eyes.

Then came the winter,
The winter in her heart,
The snakes in her hair, the gaze in her eyes.
She left me cold as a stone statue.
She walked out the door with a rose in her hair.
My mother came, made me move again.
The numbers on the page I needed to pay to live.
I begged her, she told me to leave.
I scoffed at her.

The hole in the wall, red lay everywhere
His last words, vengeance from my bloody hands
Then came the broken windows.
The rugged texture of my shell.
The frigid feel of the tiles.
Snow between my toes.

One hard year passed
Trudged through the snow filled streets
I stumbled upon the large window,
Once the gateway to my world.
I sat in the snow, remembered
My birthday, so many years ago.
The time we all sat at a round table.
My father's words of wisdom,
My uncle's firm handshakes,
The refined taste of champagne as an aperitif.
The double doors swung open,
Glimpse of trays with ham and caviar,
The clink of the glasses,
Delectable trays of Danishes and strudels,
My little gateaux with a candle in the center,
The red of the icing.

The full moon peered over the window
I blew the candle off.
One day later, New Year's Day,
Two young men found the old man.
They did not know his name or his family
They felt the heart and it was cold.
The flame had burned out.

That Night

That night
Was the end.
It was cold.
It was dark.
It was miserable.
It was over.
The end so close to the beginning.
The door shut
The chain broke.
The end under a white cover.
Snow pattered
Onto a dead end street.
The last few sentences.
She looked up into his eyes,
But he didn't look into hers.
He stood there, his hair parted.
She waited frozen, no coat to protect her beauty.
He stood in comfort, a plush winter jacket.
She waited for a while before gave up.
She forfeited her journey in the game of love.
She reached for her pocket
And pulled out something.
I looked on.
While I couldn't tell what it was
There was a certain glint in the object.
She looked one more time,
But his eyes were focused elsewhere.
She walked away
Only for him to understand that he wanted her
He called out, but she disappeared.
I saw in the distance her hand touched another.

The Sea and the Bowl

They swim the blue vastness of the ocean, circle the
globe.
They always evolve through generations,
But we evolve quicker,
Exploit them
Ingest them till few are left.
Those few are kidnapped
Sentenced to live in small pools,
Never to swim that blue vastness, never to see their
family,
Stuck here, forced to smile like young children,
Abused beyond great measures, forced to take
narcotics,
Never to have own children, never to show them the
world,
Live a life, happy to outsiders, melancholy to them.
Nobody can tell, forced to take pills to smile, to
keep the turnstiles rolling.
But soon their marketability escapes them.
One night the keepers enter to give them freedom.
They can once again swim the great blue seas.

Iron

The white of the room, the sunlight through the
window
His frail blue collared body injured at work, but
saved
By the hands of a black suited man,
From the hands of novelty, the hands of
technology.
His family took the tram across the city to see him.
The iron in the machine caused pain.

The iron in his blood, in his heart, his desire to live.
His boss lacked iron, iron hands, his hands were
soft.
He helped the sick man into the Red Cross carriage,
To let him see the light again.

The family took the tram from the blue collar
To the homes of the black suits to see him.

Badly hurt, greatly weakened,
But the iron inside of his heart would not melt,
Not to give into human pain and peril.
He lied in those white sheets for weeks,
But the iron is still in his blood, in his heart

Every minute he fights to survive, fights for life and
hope.
The iron that runs through his veins, the strength in
him.
Weeks later his eyes open to see the sun on the
windowsill,
To hear the laughs of his child, to hug her, his love,
To smile again, to laugh again, to love again.

The Twinkle in Her Eyes

Paris, a young lady, her pulchritude:
Golden hair, smooth skin and rouge.
Her heart, the white circular domes of Montmartre
like Halos.
From the bath of Holy water to
The white veil a dulcet of bells rung and the final
prayers sung.

Her brain the Quartier Latin,
The Hola of Spanish, the Hallo of German, the
Hello of English,
The move of the tassel and the reading of the Latin
diploma.

She reminisces the time she used her hands for evil,
The red of her arms, the black of her coat,
The vingtième arrondissement, a lurid place
Filled once with men dressed in white coats,
With children, who knew their mothers.

Then comes spring, and she takes a whiff of the
fresh air,
The pungent aroma of flowers in a myriad of
colours:
The ruby red of the tulips and the royal purple of the
violets,
The golden yellow of the daisies -
The Jardin du Luxembourg in late spring,
The smell of rejuvenation fills the air.

L'Opéra, the harmony of the trumpets,
Contrasted with the high, refined voice of the
soprano,

The music of life, the music of death and love.
The new lovers hand in hand, fingers intertwined as
tree roots,
Minutes after walked separate paths, as if it was just
a show.

Then the sunsets; the sky as an artist's palette:
The ravishing red, azure blue above the radiating
sun.
Her eyes glitter, La tour Eiffel.

I walk out of the tunnel and see the twinkle in her
eyes
As the full moon rises I vow to return.

A King and His Thousand Hungry

Into Morena enter men of virtue and sinners alike.
Up the hill to his highness, below the aristocrats,
Beneath them the artists, all -
Pay scant attention to the slums as they go about
their ways.

Up, crowned by fig trees he lived
He desired even a grander palace.
In a land of the impoverished and suffering
A great drought came and never left.

Imagine an audition: the king of power, the
moneymen,
The primadonna, drunk with fame,
Artists, writers, musicians, who bolstered creativity,
came
Pilgrims of love and those who lit flames of lust
The mourners journeyed from the sea of tears
The drunkard and the crazy appeared.

As the audition began a scrawny boy arrived
He tried to stop the process with all his vigour.
He was asked his name and he screamed instead,
"Empathy."
His words fell on deaf ears while he was thrown to
the curb.

The king and the primadonna became cast as a
couple.
Moneymen assigned to his trusted advisors.
The drunkard and the crazy turned into understudies
for the mourned.

Now leave this image and enter the Palace of
Morena
The king looks into the mirror and sees blue eyes,
blond hair.
But in the shanties they look out the window,
Hunger and thirst in the air, polluted water and not
hope.
The boy helps his ailing grandmother and orphaned
sister.

The fire of revolt is in their blood but the doves still
fly.
They live in misery until their corpses lie in
nameless graves.
The death of a body is but a change of clothing
In the sparrow-like journey of the soul.
As the tree loses her leaves in the winter frost,
Again rejuvenated with mother spring.

Changing Volumes

It was an era of fantasy.
Cotton candy clouds
Floated over the rainbow,
But then the rain hit the trenches,
A mass murder,
Missionaries of Christ.

The war ended the fantasy.
Forbidden fruit tasted.
Realists who worked to live
Forgot fables for cabaret.

Those kids now adults,
A lost generation,
Hidden in art and culture.

Then came a map,
Four men surrounded it
Moved boundaries to and fro.

Then came the music:
50's were jazz,
60's were cleansing and morose,
70's had us on the dance floor
Until "I will Survive".
Then appeared music from the bayou,
Synths and beats

Now, two decades
Nothing, but ear-candy
Does not give any water to the soul
Or food to the mind
Sells out is pop's adage

But 2014 is different:
Disco breathed again.
We were reminded,
That music came
From the strangest of places.
In "Cities never seen on screens"
Just like in the 70's when
Three birds visited us.

The Sunset Behind Her

To Amy W.

She had it all:
The sun shone on her,
The stars above her.
She had it all:
The world at her feet,
The Queen of soul

But then they came,
Stole her away
From stardom
With meth and alcohol

Took her from the sun
Onto this narrow path
Beside the sea of tears.
It rained everyday
Of her cries.
She tried her best to walk back
Towards the sun,
But she couldn't see it clearly
Anymore.

Every inch she took,
She thought
It was towards the sun,
But it turned to be a mirage

She had it all:
Glitz and Glamour,
Fame and Money,
But they took that all away,
Set her on this path

The further she went - the more they gave to her.
She was happy, then sad, then upset.
She was so far - nobody saw her,
Her name forgotten.
She walked until she could no more

She had it all:
Glitz and Glamour,
Fame and Money,
But they took that all away,
Set her on this path
Until she could walk no more.

They left her there
All alone, in sobs

She had it all:
Glitz and Glamour,
Fame and Money,
But they took that all away,
Set her on this path
Until she could walk no more.

She was a lost princess lured by so-called friends,
Left alone on a dead end.

The mirage was none other than a mirror.
She saw herself,
Her tears,
Her tattered clothes,
But she also saw the sun.

She had it all:
Glitz and Glamour,

Fame and Money,
But they took that all away,
Set her on this path
Until she could walk no more.

But in that sun she was no more.
There sung a new princess,
Happy and naive as she had been.
Then she saw the sunset,
Her eyes closed,
Her last words spelled out,
The dark of the night covered
The end of her life.

The Call of the Sea

He moistens her heart from the fountain of youth
only to realize it's from the sea of tears.

The glitter of the sea always alluded sailors. Many, many years ago, there was a great ship mercilessly tossed into the sea of tears. On the stern lay a high admiral dressed in a blue jacket with a pocket next to the heart. Sirens' beauty subdued him, by their glances and by their songs. They sang so beautifully, so melodically. He felt entranced and eventually fell off the deck. In the water, he opened his eyes for a moment to be met by the beautiful, lime green eyes of a mermaid. She left him there on the shore.

Several hours later his fellow men came and found him. She listened carefully as he said I remember my savior, her lime green eyes, and her diamond crown. If I can't find her, there will always be a void in my heart. She looked up to him only to find him glancing to another. As the siren came, he caressed her. The green-eyed girl left.

She then heard the song, the siren song again. She rushed to the beach only to find blood seeping from his ears. She lay there immobile on the beach. If one visits the beach, they will locate the mermaid's crown on top of the admiral's jacket in the heart pocket. She was always his queen in life and in the afterlife. And of the siren you can hear the waves hitting the shore, bringing you closer to the sea.

The Boy and the Magic Pill

Let me be met with copious ridicule, but never with
upmost fear.

He stood there alone, sobbing, afraid. He was mute, shut up by the jet set. Deemed ugly by them. The rain beat hard on him, the purple on his face, blood on his arms. Running away from life, running away from a white flash to a black eternity. Moving from that hell inside to hope outdoors, under a willow tree. All afraid, alone, with shaky hands. The silver of the dagger shone brighter than the moon's glow. But then he saw the moon getting brighter, a boat passing through the sky. Waves of change were guiding the ship towards the North Star, towards hope, towards a candle, flickering but alive. He was smiling, he ran off dropping the dagger, coming home.

The next day was similar, tears and purple adorned his face. But instead of running to the willow he stopped by the mart to pick up a magic pill to reach the streets of Neverland, to smile once. He climbed the long branches of the tree. He sat there sobbing until the moon came out and then he looked up. The moon, his boat was sailing, but in the other direction, away from the North Star, those waves weren't taking him to hope, but to misery. He looked up one last time to the Star but it was lost from his eyes, the flickering candle had blown away. Sobbing he opened the canister, took out the Magic Pill and ingested it, hoping to walk the streets of Neverland, to keep the smile forever on his face.

A Statue Through Time

I looked at the little statuette in my hand. It was my Nana's. I didn't really know her too well because she was locked in Toronto General, but she took me to the park once before. I was just five, but I remember it quite well. She brought me to the park and pushed me on the swing. We had ice cream: my favorite, chocolate with vanilla sprinkles, and she ordered pralines and cream. Then we sat on the bench. She hugged me, and we looked up at the clouds. After, my mom came and picked me up, but I visited Nana's house a couple of times. Her home was lovely, small and narrow, opening up onto a dead end street. Every single time she showed me something new, Soviet coins, Indonesian carvings, but the last visit was the most memorable.

She showed me a little Soviet figurine, a blue-eyed ceramic girl with an orange dress. But what really got me was the story behind it. Nana explained how this ceramic figurine came into her possession. It all started in a dreary apartment on the outskirts of Moscow. Her family wasn't what you called well to do, but they made ends meet. She always wanted a ceramic figurine, but her family couldn't afford it. Every single birthday she asked for one, and finally, on her tenth one, she ripped the wrapping paper eagerly to discover an elegant porcelain statuette. Then, life became tough for her.

Her dear father died, and after the funeral, she and her mom sold everything they had, just for the boat tickets. Her mother asked her to sell the figurine, but after those tears in Nana's eyes, she relented. They were only allowed one tiny black suitcase on the boat, so they left several unsold clothes and packed the figurine. After, the two made it overseas and settled in Toronto. And then came my mother and eventually me.

I always wanted to visit her in her home, but it was that phone call that stopped me. The hospital called my mom and told her that Nana had leukemia and survival was unlikely. We saw Nana in the hospital room. The figurine was sitting on the counter next to her. She tried her best to smile. I wanted to talk to her, but she fell asleep. We returned a couple more times, but every time her condition worsened.

On our last visit, she smiled and said, "Take it, I don't have much time left" in the sweetest voice ever.

I had thanked her before my mom told me to let her rest. On the way out I waved to Nana, only to see her eyes close one last time.

Then the hospital phoned my mom and explained our loss. There were a funeral and a wake, but I stayed home. I sat in my bedroom, sobbing. I took the figurine out of the box and looked at it. Her golden locks of hair, the gaze of her blue eyes. I put it on the windowsill. Every day, I look at it remembering the times I had with her, and she will always have a place in my heart.

Winter's Last Blow

The sun shivered high in the clouds. It tried to spread its magic, but winter's army forbade it. Below in the tundra lay two lovers

The night was theirs, so was the day, theirs to lose. With nothing more than an overcoat, joint and a box of matches shivering in winter's guffaw they lit the joint.

But the winter wind is harsh to the blaze. Their love, so bright and pure, the emblems, a fresh scent of a rose, the harp's song and the rugged texture of a shell, found in the parks, palaces, and canals of this great city - all froze in their war-torn minds.

They fled east from Peter's gem to the tundra where they found themselves stranded: the horses were gone and so their belongings.

The more they inhaled, the more they danced under an invisible chandelier in the golden palace, frolicked through rose gardens in spring and relished the moments spent overlooking the Neva. The ships sailed by, but those weren't the harbingers of death, but missionaries of peace: aboard, the Lord and his helpers, a couple looked up the river, and saw a path ahead, crystal clear as the water.

Then the reality hit, they were frightened, shivered as they were only humans.

They screamed, "Anna and Alexander," and the echo brought them into the storm, covered them in whiteness as their wedding day.

They held hands, still smiling, warmth left their bodies, the joint extinguished.

Inside Out

The grandioseness washed away, the derelict churches, shantytowns across the hills, those hungry, those thirsty, those lying in those dirt filled streets.

I ask one of them, veins popping out, life sucked out of him.

He responds the tide changed from the words of ancestors, the good and the evil lies in the Cerro Rico in its silver veins.

The grandioseness washed away, the derelict churches, shantytowns across the hills, those hungry, those thirsty, those lying in those dirt filled streets.

I ask one of them, veins popping out, life sucked out of him.

He responds the tide changed from the words of ancestors, the good and the evil lies in the Cerro Rico in its silver veins.

The beauty Pedro says is that a silver road, the sun radiating across the bridge, spanning to the heart of Madrid could be built, the vastness of silver that lie here.

The disgust is that the journey back could be on bones and skulls; a testament to those who died there and those who die as we speak.

The city has changed from a small Spanish colonial town to a city, shantytowns across the edges but inside those mines, deep under the skin of Cerro Rico clocks never spin, only the silver veins now bleed aluminum but the men still drain blood so much they rarely see past a half century.

I leave Pedro, the lucky one.

I walk in the rain, in the cold. I look to the right and see Cerro Rico, but my intuition leads me astray into the city's Grand Cathedral away from that vicious cycle that plagues the city, the tide that will never arrive.

The Firework and the Candle

There on a ledge in the Lee family home lay side by side a firework and a candle. The two know that May Day is happy yet sad. Celebrating the summer, mourning the loss of her father.

The two lay on a ledge, discussing life.

The candle commences "Firework, you are bursting, red, blue, green, lighting up the whole sky but I burn orange for few."

The firework responds, "I may be flashy but o, dearest candle, I live until I am lit up, to burst in the skies, a short time alas, but you live long, burning until the passage of time."

The candle then explains, "My life is miserable, to live through the beatings by rain, to live through the winter chill, the summer heat, but you are happy to light up the skies once, to have all love you, to have all in awe. You, the firework, are to help the young, to mark their milestones, to help them live, to make their May Day exemplary, to be loved, but I am to burn morosely for the dead, to help them make it through, I, a reminder of pain and misery".

In an instant come the man of the house and his lady.

On his last remark the candle states, "You are a firework bursting, green red, orange in this dull long candle-like world, be happy for your time here, it is short but vivid and blissful."   With that, the man took the firework to light it up for May Day. The lady took the candle to the cemetery to light it up next to the grave of her late father.

About the Author

A Canadian teenager has written this collection of poetry and prose over the course of last three years, and it has become the time capsule of his teenagehood.

At first, poetry was his refuge from high school, its challenges, and several unfortunate circumstances. Shortly after, the Ideas with Ink website was born as an outlet for his work the writing for him became a passion and a hobby.

He is incredibly vivid in his imagination and word choices, which draw from his experiences and aspirations. He is not scared to experiment with forms and literary devices without thinking about any accepted writing norms, making his work interesting and provoking.

He draws his inspirations from his everyday experiences, his dreams, from his worries about who he is or who will become, his exploration of his future paths and the impact that he can make in this world. All the insecurities and hopes that any modern teenager has he channels into his poetry and creates beautiful work.

He is fluent in a few languages and comes from a multicultural upbringing, which helps him to have a new fresh perspective on everyday and historical events, feelings, and emotions.

He is passionate about human rights issues, including minorities and feminism. His honesty and sincerity can appeal to any reader.

You can contact the author by e-mail at ideaswithink@gmail.com

www.ingramcontent.com/pod-product-compliance
Lightning Source LLC
Chambersburg PA
CBHW060037040426
42331CB00032B/993